The Wildlife Garde

The Wildlife Gardener

Creating a Haven for Birds, Bees and Butterflies

Kate Bradbury

WHITE
OWL

First published in Great Britain in 2017 and reprinted in 2019 by
Pen & Sword White Owl
an imprint of
Pen & Sword Books Ltd
47 Church Street
Barnsley
South Yorkshire
S70 2AS

ISBN 978 1 52671 289 9

Typeset in Ehrhardt by
Mac Style Ltd, Bridlington, East Yorkshire
Printed and bound in India by
Replika Press Pvt. Ltd.

Pen & Sword Books Ltd incorporates the imprints of Pen & Sword Archaeology, Atlas, Aviation,
Battleground, Discovery, Family History, History, Maritime, Military, Naval, Politics, Railways, Select,
Transport, True Crime, Fiction, Frontline Books, Leo Cooper, Praetorian Press, Seaforth Publishing and
Wharncliffe.

For a complete list of Pen & Sword titles please contact
PEN & SWORD BOOKS LIMITED
47 Church Street, Barnsley, South Yorkshire, S70 2AS, England
E-mail: enquiries@pen-and-sword.co.uk
Website: www.pen-and-sword.co.uk

Contents

Introduction: The Wild World On Your Doorstep

Imagine a world in which blades of grass tower above you. Where trees are giants and flowers big plates of food. In this world you dance to reveal the location of nectar, or deter predators by rolling into a ball. You might be completely harmless but wear the colours of a more sinister animal, or perhaps you started life swimming in a pool which you now only return to in order to make babies of your own. Whatever you are and however you live, all you have to do today is to eat and not be eaten, to mate and not be cuckolded.

This world exists in our gardens, attracting some of the most beautiful and magical creatures on the planet. While we're tucked up in the safety and comfort of our homes, tiny beings are hiding in our lawns and eating, mating or even sleeping on our flowers. For some of them an ornamental border is their entire universe. For others our gardens form part of a much larger habitat, spanning whole neighbourhoods and even oceans and continents.

The wonderful thing about gardens is that none of them is devoid of wildlife – every one has pollinators, birds or the odd mammal passing through. But actively creating homes for wildlife – where hundreds of species can feed, drink and take shelter – is another thing altogether.

In gardening for wildlife we help protect local species, connect with nature and learn more about the fascinating wild world on our doorstep. We

Blue tailed damselflies make a heart-shaped mating wheel.

benefit from natural pest control and improved pollination. And it's fun; when it's wet we can sit in our homes and watch frogs hop about on the patio and when it's cold we can laugh at the antics of birds squabbling over food.

But there's another reason why we garden for wildlife, and perhaps it's the most important. It's the feeling we get when we pick up a toad and look into its amber-coloured eyes; when we watch a baby blue tit visit the feeder for the first time; or when we find a lethargic bumblebee on the ground and revive her with a little drop of sugar water. It's love.

I'm no entomologist, herpetologist, ornithologist or mammalogist. I'm a gardener. But I garden as much for wildlife as I do for myself and I'm passionate about helping species that might otherwise have nowhere to live. I have a tiny north-facing garden on the south coast, surrounded by paved 'courtyards' and neglect. When I moved here it was much like the neighbours' – completely decked over and with very little wildlife. I took up the decking and transformed it into a garden. In 12 months I've counted 9 species of bird, 15 species of bee, red and blue damselflies, the common darter dragonfly, 3 or 4 species of moth and 5 of butterfly. I've found other creatures such as froghopper, the broad centurion fly and whirligig beetle – all common species, but they were absent before I took the decking up. There is still a long way to go but it has all the ingredients for a thriving wildlife garden and I know my species count will grow as the plants mature.

Our gardens are magical places in which everything is connected and all but the most alien of invaders have a vital role to play. Open your compost bin and you'll find woodlice, millipedes, giant yellow slugs and thousands of worms breaking down the waste and returning it to the earth. Take a closer at your plants and you might see the tiny larvae of lacewings, hoverflies and ladybirds making a meal of a cluster of aphids.

This book isn't a call to arms to 'Save the Aphid' or 'Love the Woodlouse', but I hope it will explain the importance of these and other creatures we gardeners have been conditioned to think of unfavourably. And, while this goes against the advice in so many gardening books, I'd like us to cherish the aphid, and the woodlouse, caterpillar and crane fly. Just a little. Just enough to keep that world outside our back door turning.

A few choice plants like this viper's bugloss can make all the difference to bees.

1

Where To Start: Creating Wildlife Habitats

Habitat: the natural home or environment of an animal, plant, or other organism

Our gardens provide wildlife habitats in their own right, but the trees and shrubs, pond, lawn and borders within them loosely represent traditional habitats such as the woodland edge, hedgerows, wetlands, scrubland and meadows.

You probably picked up this book because you'd like to share your plot with wildlife, but have you considered which wildlife? You may want to encourage hedgehogs to breed under your shed or a garden full of song birds. Perhaps you'd rather spend your summer evenings watching bats fly above you, or your summer days watching bees and butterflies visit your flowers.

Location is also a factor. Try to find out which species are living locally – whether you can attract hedgehogs, slow worms and bats, or if creating habitats for frogs and blue tits is more realistic. Most gardens are visited by bees and butterflies, but these are typically sun-loving insects. Can you give them what they need?

IT'S NO SACRIFICE

You don't need to dedicate your whole garden to wildlife, turn it into a messy tangle of brambles or stop gardening altogether. You can do as much or as little as you would like to. Gardening for wildlife can involve as little as allowing a strip of grass to grow long and tussocky, or planting a particular type of tree or a small hedge. Maybe you just want to grow the best plants for pollinators. It's your garden; it's up to you.

Opposite: Herbaceous borders provide shelter and food for anything from tiny millipedes to amphibians.
Right: Planting a mini-meadow is well worth doing if you end up with the six-spot burnet in your garden.

PROVIDE WILDLIFE CORRIDORS

It may seem obvious, but the first thing to do is physically open your garden to wildlife. You might see your plot as an individual, closed space, but many wild species see it as just one part of a much larger habitat, which not only includes your next-door neighbour's plot but could also include the gardens in the adjoining streets. Birds, bees and butterflies should easily access your garden, but what about animals that walk, crawl, slither or hop? Look around and ask yourself, 'how will frogs find my pond, how will hedgehogs access my borders?'

Providing a way in (and out) essentially increases the availability of food and shelter to garden wildlife. A hole under a fence is normally all that's needed – simply dig one on either side. You can also remove the lowest slat of a fence panel. Walls are more tricky, but it's not impossible to knock out a brick or two without damaging the structure. If you're worried your dog might run amok in neighbouring gardens, just make sure the hole is smaller than the dog – reinforce it if necessary. Hedgehogs only need 5in/13cm to squeeze through. Talking of neighbours, why not encourage them to make holes beneath their boundaries, too? A whole street of linked gardens means your local hedgehogs need never see a car again.

Opposite: A densely planted border of nectar-rich plants such as these globe thistles, provides food for pollinators as well as shade and shelter for other species including birds, amphibians and hedgehogs.
Above: The bottom panel of this fence has been removed, allowing frogs and other wildlife to travel easily between gardens.

Choosing Your Habitats

No matter how big or small your garden, you can create a variety of habitats for wildlife. Even small steps such as growing a greater variety of flowering plants or composting your garden waste can make a difference.

In creating habitats for wildlife you are providing shelter, food or water, or a combination of the three. One habitat may not meet every need of one animal, but it can fulfil some needs of many. For example, a pond provides shelter for frogs, toads and newts to breed, but it also provides drinking water for birds and hedgehogs and a hunting ground for grass snakes. Larger ponds may even attract the Daubenton's bat, which has evolved large, hairy feet for the special task of scooping insects off the water's surface.

Outside breeding season, frogs spend the majority of their lives on land, sheltering in damp,

Above Left: Simply by planting a wider variety of nectar-rich plants, we can encourage more butterflies, like this gatekeeper, to visit.
Below Left: Log pile. **Below Right:** Decking provides a more formal edge to this pond, which frogs like to shelter under in summer. Foliage at the far end also provides cover for amphibians.

secluded spots such as a log pile. They may eat other inhabitants of the log pile as well as take shelter, so this habitat meets more than one of their needs. A log pile is also a good habitat for wood-boring beetles, wood mice and wrens, and all for different reasons.

So, if you like frogs (or just want them to polish off your slugs and snails), then it's a good idea to dig a pond, but it's also worth providing habitats for them on land. But if frogs aren't high on your list of species to attract, digging a pond might still be a sensible option if you want to cater for other species.

Creating one habitat provides a piece of the jigsaw puzzle of needs for two, three, or even a hundred species. We can fit the pieces together to create a mosaic of habitats within our gardens, or team up with our neighbours to spread it over a wider area. As such, garden habitats can comprise different habitats that appeal to a number of species. You simply need to establish which species you're most interested in attracting and adjust your garden accordingly.

Above Left: To garden for toads is to garden for their food, including slugs, snails, ants, beetles and spiders. **Above Right:** Trees and shrubs provide the perfect cover for garden birds, as well as shelter for their insect food.

Shelter

I once spotted a queen bumblebee zig-zag into the garden and squeeze herself into my willow fence a second before the heavens opened. I fetched an umbrella, popped on some Wellington boots and ventured out into the rain. Wet tyres amplified the noise of traffic on the road; people ran into doorways shrieking and laughing; and I stood, a small puddle forming beneath me, rain hammering down on my umbrella, watching a bee.

I stayed for a while, barely sheltered from the rain myself, while the bumblebee snuggled up in the thatch. She had obviously been there before; parts of the fence had started to become wet but not the area

A common darter dragonfly and red admiral butterfly bask on a wooden post.

A common lizard makes a getaway to the shelter of undergrowth.

sheltering her. I went inside, occasionally returning to find her still there, before she moved on. The bad weather had lasted for hours and the bee stayed longer, but she will have eventually risen, sleepily hauling herself out of her den and off on her way. I'd never thought of the willow fence as being anything more than a barrier between me and the area beyond the garden, but now I viewed it in an entirely new light: as shelter.

Shelter includes space to hide, breed, feed and hibernate, and can be provided by anything from a pile of plant pots to a purpose-built 'hibernaculum'. Almost every part of your garden may be home to some creature or other; even a well-mowed lawn is home to leatherjackets and ants, and therefore provides food for starlings, blackbirds and green woodpeckers. Even a paved area can be home to worms, ants, centipedes and solitary bees. And a willow fence can shelter bumblebees from the rain.

Yet almost every area of our gardens can be improved for wildlife. A bare fence or wall will provide opportunities for insects to bask in the sunshine. Spiders and other invertebrates may hide in the cracks, and mason bees might make little nests for their young. But if we grow a choice selection of climbing plants up the wall it will come to life. Birds will nest in thickets of honeysuckle and ivy, bees and butterflies will feed from the flowers and moths will lay eggs on the foliage.

Shelter also includes the following.

A hedge shelters a dunnock from predators.

A Hedge

A mixed, native hedge attracts anything from nesting hedgehogs to bees, moths and butterflies, not to mention all the insects that are relied on by other species for food. As well as nesting in, and feeding from it, birds will use a hedge to dive into to escape danger; a bird table placed near a hedge will attract many more visitors than one it in the middle of a lawn with no nearby cover.

For the best wildlife potential, chose varieties such as hawthorn, beech, spindle, blackthorn, hazel, holly, field maple and buckthorn. You can add interest

It's not quite a bird's eye view, but this photo of a bird table taken from within a hedge, indicates how a bird might see this potential food source from relative safety.

by growing clematis and honeysuckle through the thicket, or planting low-growing flowers along the base. Avoid trimming the hedge until late winter and its berries will provide an additional food source when insects are in short supply, and allow leaf litter to accumulate beneath it.

A Compost Heap

A pile of rotting plant matter is a central hub where bacteria, yeasts and fungi, and worms, centipedes and woodlice help return nutrients to the soil. Because of all of the smaller creatures a compost heap attracts, it becomes a feeding ground for anything from beetles to birds, slow worms, frogs and hedgehogs.

A large, open pile is the most wildlife-friendly composting option as it's easily accessible. If you'd rather contain your heap, a slatted wooden box is the next best thing as many species can still access the goods within. Theoretically, a closed, plastic bin is the least wildlife-friendly method of composting. But it needn't be a 'closed shop'; simply raise the bin on bricks so amphibians, reptiles and small mammals can enter and exit easily. These bins can be the warmest of all, so if access is easy, you may attract a family of slow worms.

Position your heap in a sunny part of the garden and add grass clippings and other garden waste, as well as cardboard, newspaper and kitchen scraps (including eggshells but excluding dairy products, cooked food and meat). Keep the waste moist, but not waterlogged, and turn the heap to aerate it if it appears to have stopped breaking down. If you do need to turn the heap, try to do so in April, as you're less likely to disturb hibernating animals and most species won't yet have started breeding. But, regardless of your timing, make sure you check the heap beforehand and go in carefully; garden forks can easily spear frogs and hedgehogs.

A Log Pile

Replicating a habitat traditionally found in woodland, a log pile attracts a huge variety of wildlife. If you have the resources it's a good idea to use wood from local, native trees, but such logs can be difficult to get hold of, especially if you have a small, urban garden. My log pile is made from prunings from fruit trees on my allotment, half of which I leave there and the other half I carry the half mile home to my garden. It's teeming with beetles, woodlice, centipedes and other invertebrates, and may eventually attract amphibians and small mammals. If the best thing you can do is buy a bag of logs destined for a wood-burning stove then so

Above: A hoverfly takes a rest on a leaf. **Right:** If common lizards are living nearby, there's no reason why they shouldn't come into your garden if you provide shelter, food and basking sites such as wood.

be it – removed from the bag and piled in a corner they will make a wonderful habitat. Partially bury the bottom layer and fill a few gaps with fallen leaves, moss and soil to attract the greatest number of species.

A Leaf Pile

A leaf pile, too, replicates conditions found naturally in woodland, where leaves fall from trees and eventually break down to condition the soil. While they're breaking down, they provide habitats and feeding opportunities for wildlife, which in turn help recycle nutrients.

The easiest way to recreate this process is to gather fallen leaves from your lawn and sweep them under your hedge or to the back of your borders. You can also make a wire cage for your leaves using wooden posts and chicken wire. Worms, beetles and other invertebrates should still be able to access the pile easily, while a gap at the bottom will provide access to hedgehogs and amphibians.

Project: Make a Log Pile

Your log pile needn't be a messy affair – they can be attractive and interesting to have on display. If you have room, consider making two piles, one in a shady spot and another in a sunny part of the garden. Those in shady corners will remain damp and cool, appealing to beetles, woodlice and amphibians, while log piles in sunny locations will warm up and dry out quickly, providing the perfect basking spot for insects and common lizards. Any wood with bark still intact will offer nooks and crannies to squeeze into.

If you don't have a hedge or room for a large metal cage, simply gather leaves from your lawn and pop them into permeable jute sacks (or plastic bags with holes punched in), then store them behind your shed for two years. Hedgehogs and amphibians won't seek refuge in the sacks, but detritivores and their predators will still use the resulting leafmould when it's emptied out on to your borders, and it will give your soil a lovely boost, too.

TIP: Sadly, hedgehogs and toads can't tell the difference between a lovely bespoke hibernaculum and an unlit bonfire. Making the bonfire immediately before lighting or even dismantling it and reassembling prior to striking the match can literally save lives.

Project: Make a Mini Hibernaculum

Hibernaculum: the winter quarters of a hibernating animal

It's not as enticing as a great big leaf pile, but little hibernacula like this plant pot filled with leaves can provide short-term shelter for a variety of invertebrates.

Simply fill a plant pot with fallen leaves and half bury it in the ground. Pack as many leaves as you can into the pot to provide the most protection from the elements, and angle it to make sure it doesn't become waterlogged. You can provide even more protection by adding a layer of leaves or sticks above the pot.

Long, Tussocky Grass

Left unmown, a grassy strip will quickly erupt into a busy habitat for hundreds of species. Pollinators will visit flowers that may now flourish, while seeding grasses and dandelions will provide food for sparrows and goldfinches. Butterflies and moths may breed in the long grass and hedgehogs, frogs, toads and newts may use it to find food and shelter from predators.

You only need a small strip to make a difference and it needn't be unattractive. Why not make a feature of the habitat, leaving a circle of meadow

A colourful meadow (no matter how large or small) will recreate a valuable habitat that's becoming increasingly rare.

Project: How to Make a Mini Cairn

There's no real art to this, simply choose some nice rocks or large stones and pile them up in your border. Find a shaded spot so the stones don't bake whatever is sheltering inside, and leave lots of gaps for wildlife to squeeze through. Mosses and liverworts will naturally colonise the stones, but you could speed things along by adding a little soil and moss of your own if you have some to hand.

❶ Make a circle of stones and gradually start building up layers to make a pile. Aim for a sturdy triangular shape.
❷ Fill in some cracks with a little soil and pieces of moss, to give the pile a 'worn' look and encourage further moss growth.

Creating shelter can often help you as much as the wildlife. A pile of stones in your border will provide a habitat for frogs and newts, but it will also bring them closer to the slugs and snails ravaging your plants.

around a gnarled old apple tree, or cut shapes or a maze for children to run through?

How often you cut the grass is up to you, but do check the area thoroughly beforehand. You may consider raising the blade height of your mower so caterpillars and other insects can burrow into the thatch.

Spent Plants

In the wild, plants slowly break down during autumn and winter, helped along by frost and snow. Many have disappeared into the soil or the mouths of earthworms, woodlice and millipedes by spring, and new growth conceals any last skeletal remains. Yet, while plants are breaking down, they provide shelter for wildlife such as ladybirds and other insects, which sneak into seedheads and tuck themselves into hollow plant stems or among fallen leaves.

Yet, in gardens, so many insects end up on compost heap in autumn and winter, where they

Seedheads of teasel provide shelter for insects as well as nutritious seeds for birds such as goldfinches.

might be exposed to damp conditions and therefore put at risk of developing fungal diseases. By simply leaving your borders intact you can dramatically improve the chances of many species making it through to spring – not to mention earn yourself a grand view of birds eating from the seedheads you've left standing. You don't need to leave the whole border as it is – maybe you could just clear space around the edges to plant spring bulbs, or leave one untidy area concealed at the back.

Artificial Shelter

Natural nesting opportunities for birds and bees are few and far between, so by providing artificial means in our gardens we can directly improve their chances of successful breeding.

Bird Boxes

More than sixty bird species are known to use nest boxes, with blue tits being the most likely, followed by great tits and coal tits, nuthatches, house sparrows, starlings, robins and house martins. Not only do boxes provide shelter in the breeding season, but birds may also use them to shelter from the cold in winter. Swifts, house martins, house sparrows and starlings are all in decline, so provision of nest boxes for them could make a huge difference to local populations.

It's important to choose the right spot for your box, as prospecting birds are unlikely to nest somewhere with strong sunlight, a prevailing wind or where there's a lot of other bird activity (for example, if the box is too near a feeding station). It's generally advised to place the box in a north-easterly direction, but if tall buildings provide shade and shelter from the wind, then you don't need to stick to the north-easterly rule. And remember: birds don't read books. If they don't take residence after a couple of years then move the box to another part of the garden – who knows, for whatever reason the birds might like it there better, even if it's the busiest, noisiest and windiest part of the garden.

Project: How to Make a Bird Box

Bird boxes are easy to make. Each species has different nesting requirements and no one size fits all, so decide which you'd most like to cater for before you start. It's also a good idea to choose the location of the box before you get to work: do you have a fence post the box will screw into easily, or will you need to tie it to a tree? (Please don't nail it to a tree.)

The size of the entrance hole should depend on the species you want to attract:

Blue tits, coal tits and marsh tits:	25mm
Great tits, tree sparrows and pied flycatchers:	28mm
House sparrows and nuthatches:	32mm
Starlings:	45mm
Great-spotted woodpeckers:	50mm

Where to site your box:

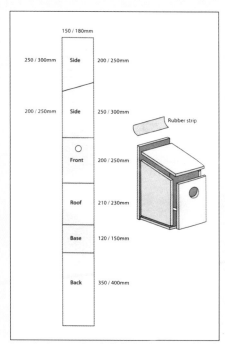

Tits:	2–4m above ground, such as on a wall, fence or tree
Robins and wrens:	less than 2m above ground, well hidden but with a clear view
House sparrows and starlings:	under the eaves of your house – add two or three boxes
House martins:	under the eaves of your house (away from starlings and sparrows)
Great-spotted woodpeckers:	1–3m high on a secluded tree, with a clear flight path

The best time to put up nest boxes is autumn, as it gives birds a few months to become accustomed to the box before nesting season. But there's no reason why you shouldn't put it up at any other time of year – it should be used eventually. The most important consideration is to fix the box securely. If you can, tilt it forward slightly, so any driving rain will not end up in the nest.

You will need:

Untreated wood at least 150mm × 15000mm
Galvanised nails or screws
Drill and wooden drill bits
Drill bit for making holes
Hammer or screwdriver
Rust-proof hinge
Waterproof material, such as rubber (I used a piece of pond liner)
Pencil, ruler

The plan shows measurements for two sizes of box. Use the larger size for starlings and great-spotted woodpeckers and the smaller dimensions for all other species. Use only untreated wood, at least 150mm thick. Treat the outside with a water-based preservative if you'd like to, but don't allow any to leach in to the box. I prefer to leave my boxes untreated, as they blend into the surroundings better and also provide a source of wood for social wasps. Make your box as snug as you can by ensuring there are no draughts, but do drill a few drainage holes in the base.

❶ Cut your wood to size according to either the large or small dimensions on the plan (make sure you stick to the same measurements throughout). If you're making a box for robins, cut the front panel to 100mm; 140mm for wrens.

❷ If required, drill an entrance hole in the front panel at least 125mm from the base. Nail or screw the pieces together. Don't nail the lid if you're making a tit box, but fix it in place with a hinge and catch, so you can clean it easily.

❸ Use tacks to attach a waterproof strip over the hinge or join where the roof meets the back panel, to prevent water entering the nest. Add a few drainage holes to the base and then firmly fix the box to its support, preferably at a slight downwards angle.

Project: Make a Solitary Bee Habitat

You will need:

An untreated wooden box (I used an old wine box)
Selection of plant stems (bamboo and sunflower stems are good)
Chopped wood or small logs for drilling into
Dry flower arranger's foam (optional)
Bracket to fix to wall or fence
Saw, drill, wooden drill bits 2–10mm diameter
Sandpaper

❶ Using a saw, cut the logs and plant stems to size, softening sharp edges using sandpaper. To attract the greatest range of species, drill lots of holes in the wood, ranging from 2mm diameter to 10mm diameter.

❷ Arrange the wood, stems and foam in the box. Once you're happy with the arrangement, make holes in the foam using a pencil or a selection of different sized pencils.

❸ Fix the box to a wall or fence in the sunniest part of the garden. You may wish to grow roses or wisteria near the box, to advertise its availability to leafcutter bees.

❶   ❷   ❸

Solitary Bee Habitats

Natural nest sites for some solitary bees include hollow stems and holes made by wood-boring beetles. All you need is a box filled with hollow bamboo and other plant stems, and wood with drilled holes 2–10mm in diameter. (If you don't have wood, try using a brick of dry flower arranger's foam and adding holes using a pencil.)

If you can, add a sloping roof to the box, otherwise fix it to the wall at a slight downwards angle so the holes don't fill with water, and choose the sunniest location possible. The first residents are likely to be mason bees, *Osmia rufa*, which nest in spring and seal their nests with mud, and leafcutter bees, *Megachile sp.*, which nest in summer and seal their nests with rose and wisteria leaves.

In autumn it's a good idea to take the box down and pop it in a cool, dry spot such as your garage or shed. This is because blue tits and other birds have learned to raid these boxes for an easy meal. Make sure everyone's happy by keeping the bees protected and topping up your peanut feeder. Just don't forget to put the bee box back in spring.

Bumblebee Nester

If you've ever watched a big, fat bumblebee zig-zagging over the ground in spring, you can guarantee it will have been a queen searching for a new nest site. Many bumblebees nest underground in old mouse holes, so a disturbance in the soil or a vague whiff of mouse will instantly be investigated, before the queen moves on, continuing her search. Eventually, she'll find somewhere she's happy with, where she'll make a little wax pot of nectar and pollen before settling down to lay her first batch of eggs.

A nest in or near your garden will bring more bumblebees, like this buff-tailed worker, to your flowers.

I've watched many bumblebees prospect for nest sites in my garden, but none has ever found it good enough. You might be more lucky, and you can increase the chances of them setting up home by creating the perfect conditions. Allowing mice and voles to nest in your garden is a good option; but you can also leave a patch of grass to grow long for carder bumblebees, which nest above ground (typically in long, tussocky grass).

Project: Make a Bumblebee Nester

This design comprises an entrance tunnel and container to house the nest and keep it dry. Bumblebees don't gather their own material so you'll need to add this yourself – pet-mouse bedding is a great choice as it gives the nest an authentic smell. While you don't have to make an underground chamber, you do have to convince the queen that the nest is below ground, so a 30cm length of hose is essential. Site your nest in a sunny spot at the base of a hedge or fence, and keep your fingers crossed.

You will need:

Plant pot, 30cm diameter
Nesting material such as dry grass clippings and moss, or pet-mouse bedding
Something to keep the nest together and off the ground (I used an old basket, but chicken wire is also good)
30cm length of hose, 5cm diameter, with plenty of drainage holes punched in
Piece of slate or broken crock

❶ Dig a shallow pit, adding a few stones for drainage if necessary. Fill the cradle with dry nesting material and place in the pit. Make sure the nest is off the ground and won't flood during heavy rain.

❷ Lay the hose down with one end in the nest and the other where you want the entrance to be. Place the upturned plant pot over the nest, making sure it doesn't kink the hose.

❸ Cover the hose with soil to conceal all but the entrance, and try to build soil around the hose to deflect rain. Keep this area weed free to make the nest more obvious to prospecting queens.

❹ Protect the nest from rain by placing a piece of slate or crock over the drainage hole of the plant pot. If a queen does set up home, you may find the workers using this as an additional entrance hole.

❶

❷

❸

❹

TIP: Bumblebees are unlikely to nest in your garden if there aren't any flowers, so grow spring-flowering plants such as willow, crocus, snake's head fritillary and hellebores. If they stubbornly refuse to nest with you, at least they will drop by for a feed.

Artificial nesting opportunities are also available for bumblebees. Many shop-bought habitats don't appear to have been designed with the nesting requirements of bumblebees in mind – prospecting queens are unlikely to spot a wooden box with a hole in the side when they're scouring the ground for tunnels smelling of mouse. That said, mouse holes are hard to come by in some gardens, so it's well worth creating something – success will be measured by how well you can mimic a rodent burrow.

Hedgehog Boxes

Providing artificial shelter for hedgehogs probably isn't necessary if you already have a log pile, open compost heap or hedge for them to nest and hibernate in, but it won't do any harm to provide additional shelter. You're not guaranteed to attract a tenant, however; some gardeners have great success with hedgehog boxes, but others aren't so lucky.

Hedgehog nests are usually found at the bases of hedges or under bramble thickets, garden sheds, log piles or compost heaps, so for the best chances of attracting residents, position your box at the base of your hedge or under a bramble thicket. Alternatively, pop it in a sheltered corner of the garden where you can cover it with a thick pile of leaves.

Food

Provision of food often automatically comes with shelter, such as a log pile, compost heap and hedge. But you can also provide food separately, starting with a few choice plants.

Plant-based Food

You probably already have bees and butterflies visiting your flowers, but you can build on what you've got by adding a wider selection for a longer period.

Plants for Pollinators

There's something almost decadent about lazing in a deckchair on a hot summer's day, half falling asleep to the sound of bees buzzing on lavender. While they're gathering food to take back to the nest, doggedly visiting flower after flower to drink nectar and comb pollen on to little baskets on their hind legs, we're just sunbathing.

But this act of lying in the sun listening to bees is one of the most important things we can do, because, if we lie in the sun and we don't hear bees, there's something wrong. At least that's what I tell myself!

Bumblebees, butterflies and moths have suffered dramatic declines in recent years, while honeybees continue to be affected by problems including Colony Collapse Disorder and parasitisation by varroa mite. Many other insects that depend on nectar and pollen – including solitary bees and pollinating beetles – are also declining.

But we gardeners can help reverse these declines, simply by growing more flowers, like lavender. It's that simple. The greater range of flowers we grow, the greater range of insects we attract, and the more

Bees and butterflies can't resist the nectar- and pollen-rich blooms of globe thistles.

we get to lie in the sun with a big smile on our face, because our work is done.

The key to planting for pollinators is to provide nectar and pollen for as long as possible. Some bees and butterflies are now active throughout winter, while others emerge from hibernation early, tempted out on warm February days when food is often in short supply. Then, in autumn, many insects need to build up their reserves before entering hibernation. So just by growing the right plants between February and November, we can dramatically improve our pollinators' chances of survival.

TIP: When choosing plants for butterflies, buy at least three of one type. A large clump of flowers is much more likely to be noticed than one on its own. Pale-coloured plants are also more easily found by night-flying moths.

A small skipper butterfly drinks nectar from bush vetch.

WHAT NOT TO GROW

As well as knowing which plants feed pollinators, it's important to recognise those that aren't so good. Many garden favourites such as begonias, geraniums (pelargoniums), petunias and pansies are bred to be resistant to disease, flower for a long time, have multi-coloured stripes or some other 'wow' factor. They survive well in drought, flower from June to the first frosts and provide a cheap burst of colour. But they don't do what they're supposed to: feed bees and butterflies. Double-flowered plants are also useless. Like a closed shop, they may be packed with pollen and nectar but no one can get to the goods.

MOUTHPARTS

You probably have little ginger bumblebees visiting your garden, and you might have already noticed that they tend to visit foxgloves and honeysuckle, while others are happier rolling around poppies or using the flat landing pads of umbels. This is to do with the length of their tongue, or proboscis. Little ginger ones, called common carders, have quite a long tongue, so can reach the nectaries of foxgloves and honeysuckle while others can't. Those with shorter tongues visit cranesbills, daisies and lavender. Butterflies have different tongue lengths as well, while hoverflies have a sponge-like proboscis, which they dab over flat, daisy-like flowers. A good rule of thumb is to grow the greatest variety of flowers possible, for the greatest number of pollinators.

NATIVE OR NON-NATIVE?

Many wildlife gardeners extol the virtues of growing native plants, while others claim it's not necessary at all. But, as far as pollinators are concerned, if the flowers have a good source of pollen and nectar, non-native plants are great. In fact, non-native plants can extend the season for pollinators, helping those that rise early in the year and go to bed late.

Don't lose sight of the fact that our pollinators have evolved a complex relationship with certain plants over millennia, so it's worth growing some native plants, especially those local to you. Some bees are more fussy than others, and so feed on a much smaller range of plants than more generalist feeders, like honeybees. These specialists aren't common garden visitors, but if you live near a nature reserve, well-managed arable area or brownfield site, you never know what might turn up. Grow a patch of red clover and keep an eye out for unusual visitors.

Further afield, some plants have evolved to be pollinated by birds. These include kniphophias, phormiums and cannas. Generalist feeders like honeybees might have a stab at feeding from them, but honeybees represent a tiny proportion of European pollinators. If you have a small garden it's best to grow plants that evolved to be pollinated by bees and butterflies as they will provide food for a greater number of species.

That said, many non-European plants are fantastic for our pollinators. These include bergamot, *Monarda fistulosa*, anise hyssop, *Agastache foeniculum*, penstemon, *Penstemon heterophyllus*, Michaelmas daisies, *Aster noviangliae*, hebe, *Phacelia tanacetifolia* and *Vebena bonariensis*.

A honeybee forages from a cranesbill flower.

A tree bumblebee gathers pollen from a Welsh poppy.

NECTAR OR POLLEN?

It's not all about nectar. For bees, pollen is just as important. Nectar is essentially sugar and water, giving life-giving energy, but pollen is rich in protein. This is mostly fed to the grubs and – for some species – the quality and amount of pollen they eat determines their size and health as adults. A grub fed with lots of good quality pollen will turn into a large, robust adult. A grub fed little or poor-quality pollen will grow up small and weedy.

Some plants produce top-notch pollen, while others are a bit mediocre. The best source comes from plants in the legume family, including the peas and beans in your veg patch. Red clover, kidney vetch, bird's foot trefoil and tufted vetch are also legumes and are therefore amazing sources of pollen.

Pollen and Nectar Plants

March–April

Apple, *Malus*
Bluebell, *Hyacinthoides non-scripta*
Broom, *Cytisus scoparius*
Bugle, *Ajuga reptans*
Cherry, *Prunus*
Crocus, *Crocus tommasinianus*
Dandelion, *Taraxacum officinale*
Grape hyacinth, *Muscari armeniacum*
Heather, *Erica carnea*
Hellebore, *Helleborus*
Honesty, *Lunaria annua*
Flowering currant, *Ribes sanguineum*
Lady's smock, *Cardamine pratensis*
Lungwort, *Pulmonaria*
Pear, *Pyrus*

Plum, *Prunus*
Primrose, *Primula vulgaris*
Pussy willow, *Salix*
Red dead-nettle, *Lamium purpureum*
Rosemary, *Rosmarinus officinalis*
Snake's head fritillary, *Fritillaria meleagris*
Sweet William, *Dianthus barbatus*
Wallflower, *Erysimum*
White dead-nettle, *Lamium album*

May–June

Alliums
Bird' foot trefoil, *Lotus corniculatus*
Bush vetch, *Vicia sepium*
Campanulas
Ceanothus

Chive, *Allium schoenoprasum*
Comfrey, *Symphytum officinale*
Cotoneaster
Echinacea
Escallonia
Everlasting pea, *Lathyrus latifolius*
Foxglove, *Digitalis purpurea*
Granny's bonnet, *Aquilegia vulgaris*
Honeysuckle, *Lonicera periclymenum*
Kidney vetch, *Anthyllis vulneraria*
Laburnum
Lupin, *Lupinus*
Meadow cranesbill, *Geranium*
Monkshood, *Aconitum*
Poppies, *Papaver, Meconopsis*
Raspberry, *Rubus*
Red campion, *Silene dioica*
Rose (single-flowered), *Rosa*
Sage, *Salivia*
Thyme, *Thymus vulgaris*
Tufted vetch, *Vicia cracca*
White clover, *Trifolium repens*
Wisteria
Woundwort, *Stachys*

July–September
Black horehound, *Ballota nigra*
Borage, *Borago officinalis*
Bramble, *Rubus fruticosa*
Buddleia
Candytuft, *Iberis sempervirens*
Cardoon, *Cynara cardunculus*
Catmint, *Nepeta*
Chrysanthemum
Cornflower, *Centaurea cyanus*

Cosmos
Dahlia (single-flowered)
Delphinium
Gaillardia
Globe thistle, *Echinops*
Hebe
Hemp agrimony, *Eupatorium cannabinum*
Hollyhock, *Alcea*
Hyssop, *Hyssopus*
Ice plant, *Sedum spectabile*
Japanese anemone, *Anemone x hybrida*
Knapweed, *Centaurea*
Lavender, *Lavandula*
Lesser burdock, *Arctium minus*
Marjoram
Mint, *Mentha*
Origanum laevigatum
Penstemon
Potentilla
Purple loosestrife, *Lythrum salicaria*
Red bartsia, *Odontites vernus*
Red clover, *Trifolium pratense*
Rock-rose, *Cistus*
Sainfoin, *Onobrychis*
St John's wort, *Hypericum perforatum*
Scabious, *Scabiosa*
Scorpionweed, *Phacelia tanacetifolia*
Sea Holly, *Eryngium*
Snapdragon, *Antirrhinum*
Sunflower, *Helianthus*
Teasel, *Dipsacus fullonum*
Thistle, *Cirsium*
Verbena bonariensis
Viper's bugloss, *Echium vulgare*

From Top Left: Bluebell, Hoverfly on chrysanthemum, Field scabious, Self heal, Bird's foot trefoil, Common knapweed, Bumblebee on lavender, Echinacea, Peacock butterfly on Buddleia.

Project: Plant up Pots for Pollinators

Container displays are ideal if you're short on space or want to add an extra splash of colour without traåmpling over your borders. They can also be great for wildlife – choose the right plants and you could have mini pollinator magnets dotted all over your garden.

These three displays are designed to provide a burst of summer colour. They're not long-term displays, but you can transfer the plants to your border in spring and use the pots to make a fresh display.

I've used three planting combinations:

Salvia 'Hot Lips'
Yarrow 'Red Velvet'
Astilbe 'Bressingham Beauty'

Lavatera × clementii 'Rosea'
Verbena rigida
Buddleja 'Buzz Ivory'

Geranium Dreamland ('Bremdream')
Salvia nemorosa 'Schwellenburg'
Sidalcea 'Party Girl'

You will need:

Pots
Plants
Peat-free, multipurpose compost
Crocks

❶ Place broken crocks over the drainage holes of your container to stop them clogging up. Half fill the pot with compost.

❷ Position the largest plant at the back of the pot, fitting the others in around it. Once you're happy with the arrangement of plants, top up the pot with compost, filling in any gaps and leaving 5cm space beneath the rim.

❸ Firm the plants well and water them thoroughly. Allow the water to drain and then move the pot to its final location.

Geranium 'Dreamland', Salvia nemorosa 'Schwellenburg', Sidalcea 'Party Girl'

Buddleia 'Buzz Ivory', Lavatera x clementii 'Rosea', Verbena rigida

Achillea millefolium 'Red Velvet', Astilbe 'Bressingham Beauty', Salvia microphylla 'Hot Lips'

Project: Make a Green Roof

If your garden is already so packed with pollinator plants that you don't have space for more, why not look to the sky? Green roofs give small gardens a little extra planting space and pollinator food that otherwise wouldn't be there. They also absorb rainfall, which can prevent water from surging into sewers during heavy rain and reduce the likelihood of flooding. Green roofs look pretty, too. In early spring, the roof of my small shed brings primroses to head height, giving me a much-needed boost when so much else is still drab and grey.

This design is for a double-pitched roof (i.e., in the shape of a triangle as you're looking head on) on a south-facing shed. It comprises an exterior frame fixed to strong internal supports, so it fits over the roof like a hat. It's planted with sun-loving sedums, which will eventually carpet the whole roof and spill out over the edges. You might consider growing a meadow if you have a large roof, or choose shade-loving plants for a north-facing aspect. And it's not just sheds that can be given a wildlife makeover; bird tables, wood stores and even bin stores can all be dressed with a little hat for pollinators.

You will need:

Wooden planks (the width will depend on your desired planting depth and if you want to conceal the roof as well for a neater finish)
Treated wooden two-by-twos
Saw
Corner brace brackets and L-shaped brackets

Tape measure

Screws

Drill and wooden drill bits

Green roof substrate (you can make your own
  using polystyrene chips and vermiculite)

Lightweight compost

Plants

Protractor

Sandpaper

Pond liner

Weed-suppressant material

Lightweight, peat-free compost

Gravel

❶ The first thing is the most important: reinforce
  your walls. All that additional wood and soil will
  put pressure on your shed, which won't have
  been designed to take the extra weight. Simply
  screw strong timber pieces into the four corners
  of your shed.

❷ Measure the length and width of the roof and
  use a protractor to calculate the angles. Use a
  saw to cut the wood to size. For a pitched shed
  like this one, you should end up with six pieces
  of wood. Sand off any rough edges.

❸ Fix the front and back pieces together, using
  corner brace brackets. Then use L-shaped
  brackets to fix them to the side pieces. This is
  your external frame.

❹ Screw wooden two-by-twos to the inside of
  the frame. These will anchor the frame, so it
  sits on top of the roof, while also concealing it.
  Calculate how many centimetres are required to
  conceal the roof and screw your batons above
  this measurement. If your roof is steep, add a
  two-by-two across the frame about half way up
  on each side, so the compost and plants don't
  slide down.

❺ Cut the pond liner to size and place it over the shed, smoothing out any creases. There's no need to glue the liner to a double-pitched roof, as the frame will keep it in place. Liners on single-pitched roofs may slip, so will need gluing.

❻ Carefully lift the frame and place it over the roof, making sure it fits comfortably. Double check that it conceals the roof and that there is adequate planting depth for your chosen plants (drought-tolerant sedums need less than 10cm).

❼ Cut a piece of weed-suppressant membrane slightly larger than the roof and loosely place it in the frame. Add substrate on top of the membrane, making sure there's a good layer at the bottom where soil and water will be at its highest concentration. Fold the edges of the membrane into the frame.

❽ Place another, smaller layer of membrane over the substrate and tuck it into the frame. Add a deep later of compost and start adding your plants. Finish with a thin layer of gravel. Water well – the water should run straight out of the bottom of the frame.

Caterpillar Foodplants

Many garden plants already support caterpillars of butterflies and moths. This is usually nothing to worry about; with the exception of large and small white caterpillars, most tend to go unnoticed. By planting a good mix of trees and shrubs, you will encourage more moths to lay eggs. This will boost the amount of food available for hungry birds, hedgehogs, bats and other predators.

The most common garden butterflies tend to have quite specific breeding requirements – some lay eggs only on large clumps of stinging nettles growing in full sun. Other garden species such as the orange-tip, meadow brown and speckled wood are easier to accommodate, so it might be worth trying to attract them instead. If you live in the right area, you may be able to lure the brimstone into your garden by planting buckthorn or alder buckthorn. Luckily, moths tend to eat a range of herbaceous plants and are therefore much more likely to breed in gardens.

While many caterpillars will be eaten by predators, others will live to pupate into beautiful adults, feed on nectar-rich plants and breed to make the next generation. All in your garden.

A stinging nettle stands out from the crowd.

Garden butterflies	Catterpillar Foodplants
Brimstone, *Gonepteryx rhamni*	Alder buckthorn, *Frangula alnus* Buckthorn, *Rhamnus cathartica*
Comma, *Polygonia c-album*	Nettles, *Urtica dioica* Hop, *Humulus lupulus* (comma)
Common blue, *Polyommatus icarus*	Bird's foot trefoil, *Lotus corniculatus*
Gatekeeper, *Pyronia tithonus*	Bents, *Agrostis* Fescues, *Festuca* Meadow grasses, *Poa*
Green-veined white	Garlic mustard, *Alliaria petiolata* Lady's smock, *Cardamine pratensis* Nasturtium, *Tropaeolum majus*
Holly blue, *Celastrina argiolus*	Holly, *Ilex aquifolium* Ivy, *Hedera helix*
Orange-tip, *Anthocharis cardamines*	Garlic mustard, *Alliaria petiolata* Lady's smock, *Cardamine pratensis* Honesty, *Lunaria annua*
Marbled white, *Melanargia galathea*	Red Fescue, *Festuca rubra* Sheep's-fescue, *Festuca ovina* Tor-grass, *Brachypodium pinnatum* Yorkshire fog, *Holcus lanatus*
Meadow brown, *Maniola jurtina*	Bents, *Agrostis* Cock's-foot, *Dactylis glomerata* Downy oat-grass, *Helictotrichon pubescens* False brome, *Brachypodium sylvaticum* Fescues, *Festuca* Meadow grasses, *Poa*
Painted lady, *Cynthia cardui*	Thistles, *Cirsium and Carduus* (painted lady) Nettles, *Urtica dioica*
Peacock, *Inachisio*	Nettles, *Urtica dioica*

Ringlet, *Aphantopus hyperantus*	Cock's-foot, *Dactylis glomerata*
	False brome, *Brachypodium sylvaticum*
	Meadow grasses, *Poa*
	Tufted hair-grass, *Deschampsia cespitosa*
Speckled wood, *Pararge aegeria*	Cock's-foot, *Dactylis glomerata*
	Common couch, *Elytrigia repens*
	False brome, *Brachypodium sylvaticum*
	Yorkshire fog, *Holcus lanatus*
Small skipper, *Thymelicus sylvestris*	Yorkshire fog, *Holcus lanatus*
Large skipper, *Ochlodes faunus*	Cock's-foot, *Dactylis glomerata*
Red admiral, *Vanessa atalanta*	Nettles, *Urtica dioica*
Small tortoiseshell, *Aglais urticae*	Nettles, *Urtica dioica*

A gatekeeper rests in grass, which it may also use to breed in.

There are so many moths that it would be hard to name them all here, but you'll get a good variety if you grow a range of these foodplants. A good field guide should help you identify them.

For moths

Apple, *Malus domestica*
Barberry, *Berberris*
Bedstraws, *Galium*
Beech, *Fagus sylvatica*
Birch, *Betula*
Blackthorn, *Prunus spinosa*
Bramble, *Rubus fruticosus*
Cherry, *Prunus avium*
Clematis, *Clematis vitalba*
Currant, *Ribes*
Dandelion, *Taraxacum officinale*
Dock, *Rumex obtusifolius*
Dog rose, *Rosa canina*
Field rose, *Rosa arvensis*
Foxglove, *Digitalis purpurea*
Fuchsia, *Fuchsia hybrida*
Hawthorn, *Crataegus monogyna*
Honeysuckle, *Lonicera periclymenum*
Hop, *Humulus lupulus*
Ivy, *Hedera helix*
Nettle, *Urtica diocia*
Oak, *Quercus robur*
Plantain, *Plantago major*
Plum, *Prunus domestica*
Primrose, *Primula vulgaris*
Privet, *Ligustrum vulgare*
Spindle, *Euonymus europaea*
Thyme, *Thymus vulgaris*
Valerian, *Valeriana officinalis*
Verbascum, *Verbascum bombyciferum, Verbascum thapsus*
Willow, *Salix*

Plants for Birds

Most insect-friendly plants are also perfect for garden birds, which need a steady supply of insects and spiders to feed their young. These are high in protein, soft and easier for the nestlings to digest than the seeds and nuts we put in our feeders. So, to provide for birds in the breeding season, simply grow plants for moths and butterflies, and tolerate the attentions of other insects on your plants, such as aphids.

In winter, caterpillars, grubs and aphids are hard to find, so birds turn to plants for sustenance. These produce nutritious seed and fruit, which help see birds through the cold months.

Birds flock to berries of plants such as guelder rose, holly and ivy, and take seeds from sunflowers, teasels, agastache and lavender. By growing fruiting plants and leaving seedheads standing, you'll not only attract more birds to your garden, but you'll also save a fortune on bird food.

Rosehips.

A female blackbird tucks into berries or rowan.

Snowberries.

Feeding birds

So, your garden is packed with natural sources
of bird food. In spring and summer, caterpillars
have free run of your plants and in winter your
herbaceous borders are packed with seedheads and
fruiting trees and shrubs. This begs the question
'if I provide natural food for birds, do I need to
supplement it with extra food?' The short answer is
yes please, because it's unlikely that natural sources
of food in your garden can support whole local

populations, and levels in the wild can fluctuate.
Feeding the birds is also an absolute joy. Position
your feeders where you can sit and watch from
the comfort of a nice armchair, and keep a pair of
binoculars to hand. It's addictive.

Traditionally it was advised to feed birds only
in winter, but we're now encouraged to do so
throughout the year. Cater for as many types as
you can – lots are used to feeding from tables and
hanging feeders but some prefer to feed from the

Fruiting Plants for Birds

Apple, *Malus*
Alder buckthorn, *Frangula alnus*
Blackberry, *Rubus fruticosus agg.*
Blackthorn, *Prunus spinosa*
Cherry, *Prunus*
Cotoneaster
Crabapple, *Malus sylvestris*
Dog rose, *Rosa canina*
Elder, *Sambucus nigra*
Guelder rose, *Viburnum opulus*
Hawthorn, *Crataegus monogyna*
Holly, *Ilex aquifolium*
Honeysuckle, *Lonicera periclymenon*
Ivy, *Hedera helix*
Mistletoe, *Viscum album*

Oregon grape, *Mahonia aquifolium*
Pear, *Pyrus*
Photinia davidiana
Purging buckthorn, *Rhamnus cathartica*
Pyracantha
Rose, *Rosa*
Rowan, *Sorbus aucuparia*
Snowberry, *Symphoricarpos*
Snowy mespil, *Amelanchier lamarckii*
Spindle, *Euonymous europaeus*
Whitebeam, *Sorbus aria*
Wild cherry, *Prunus avium*
Wild privet, *Ligustrum vulgare*
Yew, *Taxus baccata*

Seed- and Nut-bearing Plants for Birds

Alder, *Alnus glutinosa*
Beech, *Fagus sylvaticus*
Dandelion, *Taraxacum agg.*
Devil's bit, *Scabious Succisa pratensis*
Evening primrose, *Oenothera biennis*
Field scabious, *Knautia arvensis*
Greater knapweed, *Centaurea scabiosa*
Hazel, *Corylus avellana*
Hornbeam, *Carpinus betulus*
Lavender, *Lavandula*
Lemon balm, *Melissa officinalis*
Nettle, *Urtica diocia*
Oak, *Quercus*
Silver birch, *Betula pendula*

Sunflower, *Helianthus annuus*
Teasel, *Dipsacus fullonum*
Thistle, *Carduus / Cirsium*
Verbena bonariensis

A blackbird contemplates a breakfast of seeds.

ground. Don't forget to keep your bird baths topped
up. Not only does this enable birds to preen and
insulate themselves from the cold, but clean feathers
also help birds fly faster so they can escape from
predators. Birds drink from baths too.

Why you should feed birds in …

Winter

Birds don't hibernate, so forage in all conditions, stocking up on calories for energy to stay warm at night. Because day lengths are so short, smaller birds such as blue tits eat almost continually from dawn to dusk. They have a much better chance of surviving if they can fly straight to your garden to eat. Leave food out every day as birds waste energy flying to empty feeders.

Spring

Parent birds frantically gather aphids, spiders and caterpillars to feed their young, but they also need to feed themselves. Offer a quick snack of sunflower or niger seeds for them to boost their energy levels while foraging for insects. In cold, wet conditions, insects can be hard to find, so a supplementary dish of live mealworms can make a huge difference to nesting success.

As baby birds fledge, the number of birds in the garden suddenly explodes. Help fledglings fend for themselves without denying their hungry parents, by leaving out fat balls, niger and sunflower seeds. Many garden birds moult in late summer and lie low to avoid being eaten by predators. Leave food for them at the back of borders, so they can eat in relative safety.

Autumn

Birds need to be in peak condition in order to survive winter, so need a good supply of food in autumn to fatten up. Migrant birds are also starting to arrive from colder countries, adding pressure to existing food sources. Migrants are often less used to humans, so place food under the shelter of a large shrub or hedge, in which they can hide.

A niger-seed feeder is one of the best ways to lure goldfinches to your garden.

DO's AND DON'Ts OF BIRD FEEDING

Do Feed Them
- Bird seed mixes: avoid cheap mixes that contain barley, wheat, split peas or lentils, which are unsuitable for small birds
- Peanuts: preferably chopped and certified aflatoxin-free
- Sunflower seeds: black ones have a higher fat content than striped ones
- Sunflower hearts: these require less energy to eat and less waste is generated at feeding stations
- Niger seeds: popular with goldfinches
- Fat cakes and food bars: preferably in winter as products containing lard and beef suet can melt in summer
- Live or dried mealworms and dried insects
- Dog and cat food: as a substitute for earthworms in dry conditions
- Cooked, unsalted rice
- Uncooked porridge oats
- Dry breakfast cereal, preferably unsalted
- Small amounts of cake and biscuit crumbs
- Fresh coconut
- Mild, grated cheese
- Halved apples, soaked sultanas, bananas and other fruit (soak dry fruit to prevent it expanding in birds' guts)

A young blue tit tucks into a meal of fat balls.

Don't Feed Them
- Bread, especially white bread, which fills birds up without providing them with much nutrition
- Salty food, which can dehydrate them
- Cooking fat, especially turkey fat, which can smear on birds' feathers, preventing them from being able to preen or fly
- Milk, which can cause severe stomach upsets (though a small amount of cheese is fine)
- Desiccated coconut, which can swell in their stomachs and cause problems
- Mouldy food, which can cause respiratory problems
- Stale food, which can encourage salmonella virus

Diseases and parasites, like trichonomonas and avian pox, are increasing in some bird species. These are extremely unlikely to be passed on to you or your pets, but they can pass between birds via your bird table, bath and feeders. It's easy to prevent the spread of disease – simply keep the feeding area clean. Regularly scrub all items with boiling water and a dilute washing up liquid, rinse well and allow them to dry naturally, before refilling. Use a veterinary disinfectant if you have one (follow the instructions on the bottle). It's also a good idea to move the feeding station around the garden to prevent a build-up of bacteria. If you have a large garden, consider having more than one bird bath and hang feeders in separate areas to prevent all the birds flocking to one small space.

A hedgehog tucks into a dish of meat-based cat food.

Feeding Hedgehogs and Other Mammals

A hedgehog's natural diet consists of caterpillars and beetles, as well as earthworms, leatherjackets (cranefly larvae), earwigs, millipedes and slugs. On top of that, it's a good idea to leave food and water out for them in spring when they emerge from hibernation, and again in autumn before they go into hibernation and spend four to six months without food. This gives them the best chance of surviving

When supplementing a hedgehog's diet, make sure you put food out after sunset, when flies have gone for the night, and remove it as soon as possible the next day. Fly maggots can be very harmful to hedgehogs. A dish of drinking water is also essential if you have hedgehogs in the garden. Never give hedgehogs bread and milk. This can dehydrate them and make them very ill.

winter and being in a reasonable condition to breed from May onwards. You can leave food out for them in summer if you'd like to, especially during periods of dry weather when food is naturally scarce. And if you set up a feeding station complete with trail cam, you can watch them.

Supplementary Food You Can Feed Hedgehogs
- Meat-based tinned cat or dog food, especially chicken, rabbit or turkey
- Meat-flavoured cat or dog biscuits, but avoid fish flavours
- Specially designed hedgehog biscuits
- Small pieces of cooked meat leftovers such as chicken or mince
- Small pieces of mild cheese
- Chopped, unsalted peanuts
- Dry mealworms
- Sunflower hearts

Feeding Badgers

A badger's natural diet mainly consists of earthworms, but they will also eat grubs, small mammals and fruit. In dry summers earthworms retreat deep into the soil, so badgers will benefit from additional food and water. You can leave food out in a dish or scatter dry food such as peanuts over your lawn.

Supplementary Food You Can Feed Badgers

- Meat-based cat or dog food
- Seedless grapes or raisins
- Apples
- Pears
- Plums
- Unsalted peanuts
- Bread and peanut butter

Feeding Foxes

Foxes are scavengers, so will eat almost anything. But they're prone to mange, which is thought to be worse in individuals with poor nutrition. So, if you're going to feed them, try to offer them a mixed diet with plenty of protein and vitamins. Simply leave it in a dish or scatter it about your lawn.

Supplementary Food You Can Feed Foxes

- Raisins and sultanas
- Chicken – try chicken drumsticks
- Fruit, including blackberries and pears
- Meat-based dog or cat food
- Raw eggs
- Bread and butter
- Bacon
- Tuna

Feeding Squirrels

Red squirrels especially benefit from supplementary food, which helps them breed successfully, especially in areas where greys are abundant. Calcium deficiency can be a problem with reds, so avoid leaving out sweet or dried foods such as raisins and sultanas. Peanuts can also exacerbate the problem. Additional calcium can be gained from a cuttlefish bone or deer antler, if you can provide them. If you can, leave food high up in a tree so the squirrels don't have to cross open ground to access it. Feed them all year round, but only every two to three days, to encourage them to continue foraging in the wild.

Supplementary Food You Can Feed Squirrels

- Beech masts
- Hazelnuts
- Pine nuts
- Sunflower seeds
- Sweet chestnuts
- Walnuts
- Apple
- Carrot
- Pine cones

A grey squirrel rests in a rowan tree in autumn, having built its drey higher up out of danger.

WATER

Water is essential to wildlife, being something to drink, bathe and breed in. A dish of water or a few well-placed bird baths can make a world of difference. Why not go the whole hog and dig a pond?

Without doubt, the best source of water in a garden is a pond. Frogs, toads and newts, dragonflies and countless other invertebrates all breed in ponds, but they also provide a host of other species with opportunities for drinking, bathing and even hunting prey.

A frog rests in the pond shallows, sheltered by plants.

Ponds are absolutely fascinating, too: sit by one in early summer and you'll see anything from tadpoles 'schooling' like fish to mating dragonflies. Arm yourself with a fishing net and a jam jar and you can discover the magical world beneath the surface – a world of great diving beetles, water hoglice, pond snails and caddisfly larvae. Every garden should have a pond; not just because they're great for wildlife, but because they're enormous fun.

Gentle and Shallow

No matter how large or small, the most important feature of a pond is gentle sloping sides, which provide all-important 'shallows'. So many species – including frog tadpoles – are found only here, living amongst submerged plants at the water's edge. If you only have room for a small pond, it's a good idea to do away with a deeper area because small ponds don't have room for a deep area as well as gentle, sloping sides. If you dig too deeply and your pond is only 2m in diameter, your sloping sides will be too steep for most shallows-loving wildlife. And, as shallows attract a great deal more wildlife than deeper areas, a small, shallow pond is the best option for you.

If you have a large garden and can afford to give over a large area to water, then a great big pond with a deep area and graduating sides is fantastic. You'll attract a greater range of wildlife than your neighbours with small ponds, including Emperor dragonflies, ducks, coots, moorhens and bats. Toads also seem to prefer large, deeper ponds, and male frogs, eager to be the first in the water in spring, may spend winter buried in the mud at the bottom.

A pre-formed fish pond with vertical sides has fewer opportunities for wildlife than one with shallows. It won't be completely devoid of life – you

Above: A blue-tailed damselfly rests on a blade of grass, beside a pond.

Below: Skating on the water's surface is no problem for pond skaters.

A male red darter rests with his wings outstretched.

A male and female make the next generation of azure damselflies.

CONTAINER PONDS

If you have a really small garden, you don't need to dig a pond at all. In my last garden my pond' was made using an old tin bath. It wasn't teeming with wildlife but it was perfect for my rescue frogs and was also home to pond snails, water hoglice and other invertebrates. Birds occasionally bathed in it, splashing water, plants and the odd pond snail all over my patio. The bath was lined with mud and plants to recreate the shallows found in natural ponds, and I added a 'frog ladder' of stones outside the bath, for easy access. Some of my frogs ignored the ladder and just climbed the trellis behind the pond to jump in. I would have done this too, if I were a frog.

may still attract amphibians and the odd pond skater, but it won't be quite the nucleus of the garden it could be. Hedgehogs are also prone to falling in to steep-sided ponds and getting stuck. This rarely ends well.

For the best results, site your pond in a sunny spot. This will not only attract a greater range of insects but it will be more inviting to broody frogs, which prefer spawning in warmer water. Unless you

TAP WATER OR RAINWATER?

It's best to use rainwater to fill the pond, as tap water may contain chlorine and chloramines, depending on where you live, which are harmful to aquatic life. Chlorine breaks down after 24 hours, but chloramines take a lot longer. If you really have to use tap water, find out if your water supplier adds these harmful chemicals to your mains supply and act accordingly.

particularly want to attract toads, you should avoid adding fish to a pond, as they can virtually empty it of its tadpoles, nymphs and larvae. Toads are quite happy with this arrangement, however. Being slightly poisonous, their tadpoles are avoided by most fish, so they have an immediate advantage over newts and frogs; all competition for food is quickly snaffled up.

NATIVE OR NON-NATIVE?

I always stick to growing native plants in ponds, as there's then no danger of them causing damage to the natural environment if they escape the boundaries of my garden. Native plants have also evolved over millennia with our pond life; I like to think of them as the cosy old armchair that's been in the family for years – they're instantly more familiar and homely than anything foreign and fancy.

Many non-native species are incredibly invasive and some are causing havoc in the UK, clogging waterways, exacerbating flooding and removing oxygen from the water. The worst culprits include north floating pennywort (*Hydrocotyle ranunculoides*), parrot's feather (*Myriophyllum aquaticum*), New Zealand pigmyweed (*Crassula helmsii*), water-primrose (*Ludwigia grandiflora*) and water fern (*Azolla filiculoides*).

Of course, there are lots of non-native plants that don't threaten our natural environment but, by their nature, many pond plants can be pretty vigorous. So, if you choose to grow these, make sure you don't let them escape into the wild, and thoroughly compost any material you remove from the pond.

Opposite: Container ponds like this tin bath can provide a habitat for a variety of wildlife, including common frogs and some dragonflies.

Pond Plants

Pond plants provide shelter for tadpoles and other aquatic larvae, as well as a habitat for toads, newts, dragonflies and pond snails to lay eggs. There's an argument for not adding plants to your pond at all, and that it will quickly be colonised by local plants, with seeds either being carried by the wind or on the foot or feathers of a duck or other pond visitor.

This is a fine choice if you live in the vicinity of other ponds (either natural or man-made), but if you're in the middle of a city, or there's no pond for

Fallen leaves provide the perfect landing pad for mating insects, like these two pond skaters.

miles, you may prefer to add your own plants. Aim for a good mix of submerged, floating and emerging plants, which provide a variety of habitats for a variety of pond life.

TEN NATIVE POND PLANTS

1. Bogbean, *Menyanthes trifoliata*: dragonflies lay eggs in the leaves
2. Brooklime, *Veronica beccabunga*: newts lay eggs in the leaves
3. Flag iris, *Iris pseudacorus*: dragonfly nymphs use the stems to exit the water (ideal for large ponds)
4. Frogbit, *Hydrocharis Morsus Ranae*: shelters tadpoles from predators and is a good alternative to water lilies for small ponds
5. Hornwort, *Ceratophyllum demersum:* provides underwater cover for newts, frogs and toads and absorbs excess nitrates in the water, preventing the spread of algae
6. Marsh marigold, *Caltha palustris*: toads lay spawn around submerged stems and dragonfly nymphs use them to climb out of the pond
7. Starwort, *Callitriche palustris*: offers surface protection for tadpoles and absorbs excess nitrates in the water, preventing the spread of algae
8. Water forget-me-not, *Myosotis scorpiodes:* newts lay eggs in the leaves
9. Water lily, *Nymphaea alba*: newts shelter under them and honeybees use them as landing pads through which to drink water
10. Water soldier, *Stratiotes Aloides*: protects tadpoles from predators and a good alternative to water lilies for small ponds

FIVE NON-INVASIVE, NON-NATIVE PLANTS

1. Blue pickerel, *Pontederia cordata*: provides late flowers for pollinators (marginal)
2. Dwarf rush, *Juncus ensifolius*: ideal for small ponds (marginal)
3. Himalayan marigold, *Caltha Palustris var Alba*: similar to marsh marigold, but ideal for small ponds (marginal)
4. Nymphaea 'Hermine' (cultivar): provides cover for tadpoles, ideal for smaller ponds
5. Water hawthorn, *Aponogeton distachyos*: provides surface cover for tadpoles

Project: Dig a Small, Shallow Pond

Before you start, choose a site for your pond and work out how much space you have and whether you want a formal pond or a more natural looking one. Informal, natural edges such as grass tend to be better for wildlife as they're closer to what would normally be found in the wild. Simply laying turf is one of the easiest ways to edge a pond. It might turn yellow at first, but it should survive, and the shallow root run will prevent the grass from growing too long.

This pond has a diameter of just 2m and is edged with grass. I dug it into a south-facing border on the edge of the lawn, so on one side I was able simply to pull back a section of lawn and bury the liner beneath it. I laid turf to keep the rest of the liner in place, and replaced the border plants I had dug up to make the pond, to create a densely planted habitat to protect emerging frogs.

You will need:

Butyl liner and underlay (if you don't want to buy underlay you can use sand or an old carpet)
Spade, spirit level, plank of wood
Something to measure the pond with (I used string and a piece of bamboo)
Pond plants (optional)

Turf to hold the liner in place
Gravel (optional)
Large stones
Log

❶ Start by marking out the shape. I made a basic circle using a piece of bamboo and a length of string, but you could use sand or a hosepipe to mark yours. You don't have to make a circle, be as creative as you like.

❷ Start digging from the centre, working your way out. Don't dig any deeper than 30cm. If you're going to add plants, create a shelf for them along one side, making sure the shelf is wide enough to accommodate all of your planting baskets.

❸ Level the edges of the pond, making sure there are no steep ridges, and remove any sharp stones you find as you go around. Lay a plank of wood across the pond and use a spirit level to check that the sides are even.

❹ Cut the underlay and liner to size, cutting more than you need. Lay the underlay down first (add two layers if you have enough material), smoothing out any lumps or bumps. Then

add the liner. Use a soft broom to get into any corners and remove creases.

❺ Replace turf if you have dug into a lawn, or cut turves to size and position them around the edge of the pond to keep the liner in place. Finish off with anything from washed gravel, large stones or a log – whatever suits you.

❻ Add water from your water butt or wait for rain. Once the pond has partially filled, add your plants. Pot up marginals in planting baskets topped with gravel, and place them on the shelves. Add floating and submerged plants to the water.

Make a Bog Garden

Bog gardens are also good for wildlife, as well as giving you the opportunity to grow some really exciting plants. They're a great option if you have a small garden as you can create habitats for amphibians and food for pollinators, birds and bats in one area. You can either make one to complement your pond or add one in its own right. And what is a leaky pond, but the perfect excuse to create a bog garden?

Simply create the bog garden in the same way you would create a pond, only much shallower (about 20cm deep). Pierce a few holes in the liner and add a layer of gravel, for drainage. Then just choose your plants.

Ten bog garden plants

1. Devil's bit scabious, *Succisa pratensis*
2. Hemp agrimony, *Eupatorium cannabium*
3. Lady's smock, *Cardamine pratensis*
4. Marsh mallow, *Althaea officinalis*
5. Meadow sweet, *Filpendula ulmaria*
6. Pennyroyal, *Mentha pulegium*
7. Purple loosestrife, *Lythrum salicaria*
8. Ragged robin, *Lychnis flos-cuculi*
9. Teasel, *Dipsacus fullonum*
10. Water avens, *Geum rivale*

BIRD BATHS

A bird bath makes a fantastic addition to gardens, even if you already have a pond.

Not only do birds drink from them, but they use the water to clean their feathers. Hedgehogs also drink from bird baths if they can access them, while frogs might sit in them (although this isn't particularly sensible, as quite a few birds eat frogs). Honeybees, wasps and other insects also drink from bird baths, so add a few stones around the edge to enable them to exit easily. If you have space, dot a few baths around the garden. Choose pedestal baths as well as those that sit on the ground. Baths that hang from trees are also popular.

A dunnock cautiously enters the water to take a drink and clean its feathers.

PEST CONTROL

In the Hanyuan County of Sichuan, China, fruit growers hand pollinate their pear trees. The process is labour intensive and costs a lot of money, but the farmers have no choice; if they didn't pollinate the trees by hand, they wouldn't have any pears. Not only have pesticides wiped out natural pollinators in the area, but many local beekeepers have moved their hives out of the county for fear of losing their bees, due to continued pesticide use.

I'm sure we've all stepped out into the garden to find a tray of seedlings reduced to little slimy stumps by slugs or snails, or picked up a special plant to find it no longer has any roots, thanks to the voracious appetite of vine weevil larvae. At these times, it can be difficult to do anything other than reach for the chemicals. But chemicals do so much more than remove one or two specific troublemakers from the garden. At best, they take a few other creatures out as well as the intended recipient; at worst, they knock the whole garden ecosystem out of kilter.

Bug sprays are used to kill a range of insects, including aphids, mealybugs and lily beetles. But if you zap a cluster of aphids on your broad beans, you're also likely to take out their insect predators – the ladybirds and hoverflies. Most ladybirds and hoverflies breed only once a year, whereas aphids breed constantly throughout summer (in fact, some can reproduce without mating). So if you kill the aphids, hoverflies and ladybirds, you're actually creating the perfect conditions for aphids to breed without any threat from predators at all. Then you take on the role of the predator; regularly spraying the aphids to keep numbers down. You become reliant on the bug spray, spraying more and more to keep the aphids in check. It's a vicious circle that will ultimately only lead to one thing: pollinating your crops by hand.

A butterfly drinks nectar while a bumblebee gathers pollen.

It's not just bug sprays. Hang a piece of yellow sticky fly paper in your greenhouse and you'll catch and kill anything from whitefly to hoverflies, bees and butterflies, even small birds. Scatter slug pellets around your hostas and you run the risk of harming the song thrushes and hedgehogs that eat slugs and snails. Add a vine weevil drench to your container-grown plants and you may see fewer bumblebees in your garden next year. On top of that, all of these 'pests' are food for some creature or other. It's why they exist.

This all sounds very dramatic. And it might seem silly comparing the effects of widespread pesticide use in China with small-scale spraying in our ornamental borders, vegetable patches and greenhouses. But pesticide use is rife the world over, covering large areas of farmland. This, surely, is reason enough not to use them in our gardens; together, we can create the biggest nature reserve in Europe.

Since the 1990s, a new group of pesticides has been used that has been linked to bee deaths, particularly Colony Collapse Disorder. Known as neonicotinoids, these pesticides are systemic, meaning they're absorbed into every part of the plant. The chemicals are often applied as a coating to seeds and, as the plants germinate and grow, they absorb the chemical and provide protection against insects that eat the leaves or roots. Unfortunately, the chemicals are also taken into the pollen and nectar of the plants' flowers. While the chemicals are present in extremely small doses, a bee can visit 1,000 flowers a day, collecting pollen and nectar to turn into honey, which is fed to the grubs. One colony of bumblebees can contain up to 300 workers, while a honeybee hive houses up to 40,000 bees. If each worker visits 1,000 neonicotinoid-treated flowers every day, then very quickly you have a large concentration of pesticide residue back at the hive or nest.

A study conducted in Scotland in 2011 showed that bumblebee nests exposed to neonicotinoids produced 85 per cent fewer queens than those not exposed to the pesticides. The bumblebee lifecycle is annual; daughter queens are produced in summer before the original queen and workers die. The new queens mate and build up their fat reserves before hibernating, and then each one starts a new nest in spring. In summer each queen produces her own daughters to continue the cycle the following year, before she and the rest of her nest die.

The six months between mating and starting a new nest are already perilous for daughter queens and many don't survive. They might not be able to build up enough fat reserves so they die of starvation, or they may be disturbed during winter, or frozen to death or even flooded, if they don't choose a good hibernation spot. A reduction of 85 per cent in the number of daughter queens could mean that no queens from the original nest produce a new colony the following spring. Ultimately, this could lead to extinction.

Another study, conducted in France, showed that honeybees exposed to neonicotinoids were less able to navigate their way back to the hive. This means less food is produced for the grubs, lost workers die and the colony gradually dwindles in size (under normal circumstances worker bees live for just a few weeks and are replaced by the next brood). This could explain, or at least contribute to, the phenomenon known as Colony Collapse Disorder, where beekeepers suddenly find their hives deserted.

Since 2011 there have been scores of studies adding more momentum to the case for a permanent ban on neonicotinoids. There's evidence to suggest they harm a range of other species such as butterflies, bats and birds. They're found in soil and waterways. As more research is done the jigsaw puzzle is being completed: neonicotinoid pesticides harm wildlife at the bottom of the food chain, and so therefore the impact of them will be felt further up it. The chemicals also live in the soil after the plants have died; some studies have shown wildflowers growing next to sprayed crops containing dangerous levels of neonics.

In 2013 The European Union (EU) restricted commercial use of three types of neonicotinoid pesticide on flowering crops for two years. At the time of writing this has been extended: the use of neonics is prohibited on flowering crops across the EU, but France, Germany and Italy are proposing more comprehensive bans on their use on other crops too. In contrast, the UK government seems keen to overturn EU restrictions. It's worth noting that, since the British referendum to vote to leave the EU, it's unclear whether any EU restriction would hold post-Brexit. However, some neonicotinoid pesticides are still contained in bug sprays for the home gardener.

Bumblebee expert Dave Goulson says: 'Neonicotinoids have proved to be highly persistent compounds, which have contaminated our soils, hedgerows, wildflowers and streams. There is a growing body of evidence that they may be harming not just bees, but also aquatic insects, butterflies and insect-eating birds. It would seem prudent to stop all uses of these neurotoxic compounds.'

Regardless of what our governments and the manufacturers say or what happens after the UK has left the EU, it's clear that use of these pesticides is linked to bee declines. While we may not be able to control what happens in the wider countryside or political arena, we can guarantee our gardens remain safe for bees and other pollinators simply by not using pesticides. We can also buy as much organic food as possible, thereby increasing demand for food grown without the use of harmful chemicals.

Alternatives to Using Pesticides

As we already know, ladybirds and hoverflies eat aphids, and many garden birds feed them to their young. Caterpillars, too, are eaten in their thousands every spring.

I rarely see aphids in my garden and caterpillars don't get much opportunity to eat my plants when the great tits are breeding. I used to have a problem with vine weevil but I don't anymore, thanks to the frogs, which also do a brilliant job of keeping the slug population in check. But I wish something would eat the snails. I find the damage they cause frustrating, time consuming, even heart wrenching, but that's snails; they eat your plants.

My favourite way to deal with snails is to take them on holiday. I gather them up in a bucket and carry them to the wildlife area in the local park. Some will no doubt thrive and breed, while others will be eaten by song thrushes and other predators, which rarely come into my garden.

The main thing is to relax. If you see aphids on your broad beans, don't panic. Don't squish or spray immediately, but sit back and see what happens. The predators will likely find them in due course. If, after a couple of weeks, there are still no predators picking off your aphids, then go ahead, squish a few. But make sure there's still enough to feed the more well-behaved wildlife you do want to attract.

Organic Methods of Pest Control

Slugs and snails
- Conduct regular night-time inspections and remove slugs and snails by hand
- Sink cups of beer into the ground, which slugs and snails will be attracted to and fall into and drown (ensure the traps are proud of the soil's surface to stop ground beetles from falling in)
- Leave piles of bran or oatmeal around your plants, which expand in the stomach and can lead to a rather unpleasant death

TIP: One of the easiest ways to control greenfly and blackfly is grow a patch of nettles. This will attract the nettle aphid, *Microlophium carnosum*, which emerges earlier than other aphids, giving ladybirds a head start on potential infestations in your garden.

- Apply nematodes (naturally occurring slug parasitoids) to the soil in spring and autumn to reduce slug populations without harming other wildlife
- Create hiding places for slugs and snails near vulnerable plants, which you can check daily. Simply leave out a piece of slate or broken plant pot to create damp, dark shelter
- Install physical barriers, such as copper rings and plastic cloches, around your plants
- Use rings of grit, crushed egg shells or spent coffee grounds to deter molluscs and refresh them regularly, especially after rainfall.

Aphids

You can use an organic soap spray, squish them with your fingers or blast them with a jet from your hose, but try to avoid doing so if you have nesting birds in the garden and do check that ladybirds and hoverflies haven't already moved in.

Caterpillars

Remove them by hand and place them on the bird table. Alternatively, you can transfer the caterpillar to another host plant (elephant hawk-moths, for example can be moved from fuchsias to rosebay willowherb).

The crocodile-like ladybird larvae (left) takes a rest while aphids (right) gather on the growing tips on a young rose leaf.

TIP: If you've always used pesticides and suddenly stop, you're going to experience an explosion of aphids and other pests before the predators return to keep them under control. Unfortunately, this is inevitable and necessary, as it will take time for the natural balance of your garden to be restored. Other factors, such as the location of your garden and the weather can also play a part in the fate of your plants. For example, if you live in a city you may not have a local population of hedgehogs to eat your slugs and caterpillars, and a wet summer is all that's needed to ensure you're overrun with slugs and snails. But your garden will right itself in time. In the meantime, use organic methods of control, but make sure you don't remove all pests, otherwise they will be no food for the frogs, birds and hedgehogs you want to attract. Sometimes, you'll need to tolerate a little plant damage.

Vine weevil
- Apply nematodes (naturally occurring slug parasitoids) to containers in spring and autumn to kill the larvae without harming other wildlife
- Check vulnerable container-grown plants regularly for signs of eggs or larvae, removing any you find
- Remove adults as and when you find them

Lily beetle
In many parts of Europe, there are four parasitic wasps to keep lily beetle numbers under control, but far fewer outside its natural range (there's just one in the UK). The easiest way to get around the problem is to stop growing lilies, but if you don't want to do that, you'll need to regularly remove adults and larvae by hand.

2
Introducing …

So you've created corridors, planted flowers, made a log pile and dug a pond, and the wildlife is flooding in. But what on earth are all these creatures, what do they 'do' and how can we make their lives even more comfortable?

BIRDS

Birds are the most obvious, and colourful, garden visitors. If you have a good mix of trees and shrubs, natural food and a feeding station complete with bird bath and a selection of supplementary food, you should expect around thirty different species.

Identifying most garden birds is easy. Start in winter if you're a complete beginner, as all birds will by then have their adult feathers, making each species more distinguishable. They will also be concentrated around your bird feeders, so you can sit in the warmth of your home with a pair of binoculars and a field guide, learning the different colours and behaviours of each species.

LOOK OUT FOR: ground feeders such as robins, blackbirds, wrens and thrushes, and tits and finches, which are happy visiting hanging feeders.

Ten things to do for birds

1. Mulch borders with leafmould
2. Mow your lawn at different lengths – short for blackbirds and starlings, longer for insect-eaters such as sparrows, seed eaters such as chaffinches, and vole eaters such as owls
3. Plant a variety of shrubs and trees, or a hedge, including leafy broad-leaved trees to attract insects, and those that produce fruit
4. Cover walls and fences with a variety of climbing plants
5. Make a log pile
6. Put up bird boxes
7. Dig a pond and/or install a bird bath
8. Grow a variety of caterpillar foodplants (see p. 27 for details)
9. Provide supplementary food all year round (see p. 35 for details)
10. Leave dead wood on trees

Left: Blue tits will be attracted to peanut feeders.
Opposite: The call of the male blackbird may be the first thing you hear each day in spring. If he doesn't find a mate he may sing throughout summer.

1. BLUE TIT, *Cyanistes caeruleus*

The blue tit is a gorgeous mix of blue, yellow, white and green. It eats insects, spiders and berries as well as peanuts, sunflower seeds and fat-based products. You might spot them picking aphids, one by one, off clematis stems or hanging upside down from tree branches. The male and female have the same colouring but fledglings look like they've had a lemon wash – their feathers are duller and tinged with yellow.

Blue tits are common inhabitants of nest boxes. The female builds her nest from moss, wool, grass and hair, before laying between five and sixteen smooth, white eggs with purple or brown spots. Breeding pairs tend to have just one brood a year, which they incubate for twelve to sixteen days. The young fledge after sixteen to twenty-three days.

HOW TO ATTRACT THEM: install a nest box and plant deciduous trees, to boost numbers of insects, spiders and caterpillars.

2. GREAT TIT, *Parus major*

The great tit is bigger than the blue tit, green and yellow with a distinctive black stripe down the breast (this is more prominent in males – males with wide stripes are more dominant, and attractive to females). Like blue tits, they eat insects; particularly caterpillars, beetles and flies, and they take peanuts, sunflower seeds and fat-based products from feeders. In spring they feed caterpillars, spiders and insects to their young.

Great tits nest in holes in trees and nest boxes, using moss, grass and down, hair and feathers. The female lays up to two clutches of eggs per year, of five to twelve eggs per clutch. The white eggs are smooth and glossy with purplish red spots. They're incubated for twelve to fifeen days and the young fledge after sixteen to twenty-two days.

HOW TO ATTRACT THEM: install a nest box and plant as many deciduous trees as you can.

3. LONG-TAILED TIT, *Aegithalos caudatus*

The long-tailed tit is absolutely adorable, like a little flying badger. Small, fluffy and pinkish with a really long tail, adults gather in large family groups in winter, egging each other on with a little 'deet deet' to fly, in turn, from one tree to another. They're predominantly insect eaters, taking moth and butterfly eggs, bugs and small insects, but some have recently learned to use garden feeders.

The nest takes three weeks to build and is an elaborate ball of moss, spiders' webs, lichen, feathers and hair. The female lays up to twelve smooth, glossy white eggs with purple-red spots. Eggs are incubated for thirteen to eighteen days and the young fledge from fourteen to eighteen days. Family members that don't breed successfully often chip in to help those with large broods.

HOW TO ATTRACT THEM: plant trees and dense, thorny bushes for them to shelter in and find food.

4. BLACKBIRD, *Turdus merula*

The blackbird has one of the most beautiful songs of all garden birds: a rich, fluty call that often lasts throughout summer. Only the male is black; the female is a dull brown, often with spots and streaks on her breast. Juveniles are also brown, and young males don't develop a bright orange beak until the following year.

Blackbirds eat worms and insects from lawns and borders. In winter they eat windfall fruit and berries, and turn leaves over in search of grubs.

The nest is made using grass, twigs and mud. The female lays up to five smooth blueish eggs with reddish-brown spots. Eggs are incubated for two weeks and fledglings emerge after a further two weeks. Nesting pairs can have as many as three broods per season.

An adult male blackbird (identified by its orange beak) perches on a tree.

HOW TO ATTRACT THEM: make leaf piles or mulch borders with leafmould, and leave windfall apples on the ground.

5. HOUSE SPARROW, *Passer domesticus*

The sparrow is declining in Europe, especially in urban areas. This is possibly due to loss of nesting sites, changes in agriculture and a lack of insects.

The male has a grey crown, and black stripes around the eyes and just below the beak (bib). The paler female lacks the grey crown, black bib and eye stripe, and has a straw-coloured stripe behind the eye. Adults eat seeds, but need insects to raise their young.

They live in colonies in holes in buildings, or nest boxes. The nest is made with leaves, grass and even rubbish. Nesting pairs can have up to five broods of three to five speckled white eggs per year, which are incubated for eleven to fourteen days. Fledglings emerge after eleven to nineteen days.

HOW TO ATTRACT THEM: boost insect numbers by letting an area of grass grow long, plant a deciduous tree or hedge, and make a log pile.

6. SONG THRUSH, *Turdus philomelos*

To have a song thrush in the garden is a wonderful thing, not just for its beautiful song, but its appetite for snails. It's smaller than the blackbird and less upright when standing. Adults are brown, with arrow-like markings on their golden-cream breast. They eat worms, insects, berries and snails. If you're lucky, one may use a stone in your garden as an anvil to open snail shells.

The female makes her nest in a tree or bush, from grass, twigs and earth, and lays up to five blue eggs with black spots. Eggs are incubated for ten to seventeen days and fledglings emerge up to seventeen days after hatching. Song thrushes tend to have up to three broods per season, but if there's plenty of food around, they can have up to five.

HOW TO ATTRACT THEM: keep an area of your lawn short and plant fruiting shrubs, such as holly.

7. SPARROWHAWK, *Accipiter nisus*

The sparrowhawk is a magnificent creature, despite its appetite for small birds. While some people may find the sight of sparrowhawks upsetting, they're sign of a healthy bird population.

Mostly grey in colour, adults have a grey hooked beak, a pale, barred underbelly and spindly yellow legs. Females are bigger than males, so prey on larger birds, including thrushes, starlings and pigeons, while males stick to tits and sparrows. Small mammals may also be taken.

Nests are made from twigs and built in trees or large, thorny bushes. The female has just one brood, laying up to six smooth, blueish eggs. Eggs are incubated for up to forty-two days and the young fledge after a further twenty to thirty days.

HOW TO ATTRACT THEM: create a healthy garden bird population. If you'd rather deter them, place feeding stations near a dense hedge, for small birds to escape to quickly.

8. GREENFINCH, *Carduelis chloris*

The greenfinch's wheezing song is unmistakable, sounding a bit like a tired, contented sigh. Only the male is green; the female is more of a dull brown with green eye patches. Both have yellow-green edges to the wings. Adults mainly eat seeds, but will also take berries and rosehips in winter. They feed insects and spiders to their young.

Greenfinches are unlikely to use nest boxes and often nest in small colonies in dense shrubs and conifer trees. The nest is made from twigs, grass, moss and hair. Nesting pairs usually have two broods per season, with the female laying up to six smooth, glossy white eggs with blackish markings. Eggs are incubated for eleven to fifteen days and fledglings emerge from the nest after up to eighteen days.

HOW TO ATTRACT THEM: fill feeders with sunflower hearts and plant dense shrubs and hedges for them to nest in.

9. CHAFFINCH, *Fringilla coelebs*

You're most likely to see chaffinches foraging on the ground for insects, or under the bird table for spilt sunflower seeds, but they may also visit hanging feeders. The male is chestnut brown with a distinctive pink underbelly and the female is more of an olive-brown with grey-brown belly. Both have two white bars on each wing.

The nest is made in trees and shrubs and is a beautiful cup of moss, grass and feathers bound with spiders' webs. It's lined with feathers and wool and then finished off with lichen and flakes of bark. The female lays up to two broods of four to six smooth, glossy, light blue eggs with purple-brown blotches. Eggs are incubated for up to sixteen days and the young fledge after a further eleven to eighteen days.

HOW TO ATTRACT THEM: provide lots of dense, shrubby cover and as many trees as you have space for.

10. WREN, *Troglodytes troglodytes*

Small, brown and fidgety with a cocked tail, the wren dashes about eating spiders and insects, probing crevices with its long, thin beak. It can suffer in winter when food is in short supply, and large numbers may squeeze into bird boxes, for warmth.

In spring, the male makes several nests of leaves, moss and grass for the female to choose from. Once the female has picked her favourite, she decorates it with feathers. She then lays five to eight smooth, glossy white eggs with reddish spots, which she incubates for twelve to twenty days. Wrens can have two clutches per year, but the male may have more than one female in his territory (well, if he's made all those nests …). Fledglings emerge after fourteen to nineteen days.

HOW TO ATTRACT THEM: provide lots of potential nest sites for males to woo a female or two, and make a log pile.

A wren perches on a garden fence. Note its cocked tail and alert stance.

MAMMALS

You'll find mammals anywhere, including under the shed or among piles of logs or leaves, high up in trees or low down in tussocky grass. As long as they can enter and exit your garden easily, and have space to nest, shelter and feed, they will be quite at home. Common species include squirrels, bats, hedgehogs and wood mice, but you may also attract badgers and foxes. For some gardeners, rabbits, deer and moles are seen as pests, but others welcome them with open arms. Few gardeners are so hospitable to rats, but we'll get on to them later.

Identifying most mammals is easy. It's simple telling a fox apart from a badger or a rabbit apart from a hedgehog, but learning the difference between a vole and a wood mouse is more difficult. If you have a lot of bats flying over you garden, you may want to invest in a bat detector to help you identify your pipistrelles from your Daubenton's.

LOOK OUT FOR: visible tracks, or signs. All animals leave poo, trapped fur, footprints or the remains of food, so, with a bit of practice, you'll be able to work out what's visiting.

Ten things to do for mammals
1. Make log and leaf piles
2. Create access holes at the bottom of your fences
3. Grow nectar-rich plants, to attract insects
4. Only build bonfires immediately before you light them
5. Keep pea netting off the ground
6. Let a patch of grass grow long
7. Compost kitchen and garden waste
8. Avoid using slug pellets
9. Plant a hedge and include species like hazel and honeysuckle
10. Dig a pond

1. HEDGEHOG, *Erinaceus europaeus*

The hedgehog is almost entirely covered in spines, although the belly and chest are covered in a coarse brown fur, which is visible as a sort of underskirt. They can be quite noisy little things, often grunting and snuffling like little, prickly pigs.

Adults nest in compost bins, under sheds, in leaf piles and clumps of ornamental grass. They also hibernate in these places, typically between November and March. Nocturnal, they travel long distances to mate and find food, which includes caterpillars and beetles, earthworms, leatherjackets, earwigs and slugs. They also eat food we leave out for them (see p. 37 for details).

Mating takes place from April onwards and up to five young are born per litter, usually between May and September.

HOW TO ATTRACT THEM: plant a hedge and make leaf piles for them to nest in, and ensure they can enter and exit your garden easily.

2. FOX, *Vulpes vulpes*

The red fox is all pointy face, burnt-orange coat, white chest and big bushy tail. It's typically found in rural areas, but the so-called 'urban fox' has recently adapted to live in some towns and cities – you might find a family living under your shed.

Foxes emerge at dusk to forage on anything from insects, earthworms, fruit and berries, to birds, small mammals and carrion. They will eat scraps left by humans and may even rummage through your bins to access food you've thrown away.

Mating takes place in late winter. The mating call can be quite terrifying if you've not heard it before – a sort of wild shriek. Around five cubs are born between March and May.

HOW TO ATTRACT THEM: ensure they can access your garden. If you'd rather deter them, block entrance holes to potential nesting sites and reduce the amount of food you throw away.

3. BADGER, *Meles meles*

The badger is short and stocky, with silvery-grey fur and gorgeous black and white facial markings. It mostly lives in woodland in family groups, occupying underground setts in territories that are marked by partially buried 'latrines'. Nocturnal, badgers emerge at dusk and spend the night foraging for food. Breeding takes place all year round and up to six cubs are born per litter.

The badger's diet mainly consists of earthworms, but they may also eat frogs, rodents, hedgehogs, birds, eggs, lizards, insects, bulbs, seeds and berries. In summer, when rainfall is scarce and worms retreat far below the soil's surface, badgers may dig up bumblebee and wasp nests to eat. They're also partial to digging up lawns to eat chafer grubs.

HOW TO ATTRACT THEM: ensure they can access your garden and leave food out for them. If you'd rather deter them, consult your local badger group for advice.

4. WOOD MOUSE, *Apodemus sylvaticus*

The wood mouse can be told apart from the house mouse by its sandy brown coat, long tail, big ears and big eyes (the house mouse, *Mus musculus*, is grey, with a shorter tail, smaller eyes and ears).

They mostly eat seeds and fruit, but also insects and small snails. Nests are made in underground burrows, sheds and compost heaps, and lined with leaves, moss and grass. The female gives birth to up to three litters of around nine babies per year, and the young are ready to reproduce within three weeks.

But their lifespan can be as little as three months, and owls, kestrels, foxes, badgers, weasels and cats eat them. Wood mice are also firmly entrenched in the wider garden ecosystem: old burrows are used by nesting bumblebees and other species may hibernate in them.

HOW TO ATTRACT THEM: provide dense vegetation and access to your compost bin.

5. VOLE, *Microtus agrestis* and *Myodes glareolus*

Voles have a thick coat, furry ears, short tail and a rounded, whiskery snout. The most common garden visitor is the chestnut-coloured bank vole, which eats fruit, nuts, snails and small insects, hazlenuts and blackberries. Bank voles live at the base of hedges and beneath shrubs.

The field vole inhabits larger, rural gardens where lawns are left unmown. Its whole life revolves around grass, which it eats, shelters and nests in. It spends most of its time hiding from predators, but look out for well-worn paths in long grass, piles of cut grass and greenish (grassy!) droppings.

Both species breed between March and December, having up to six litters of four or five young per year. Field voles tend to nest above ground, while bank voles nest below ground.

HOW TO ATTRACT THEM: let an area of grass grow long, create patches of dense vegetation and a log pile.

6. BAT

Bats are the only flying mammals. They can see, but echolocate to fly and feed at night, sending out shouts and listening to the returning echoes to create a sound picture of what's around them. These shouts are inaudible to humans, but you can hear them using a bat detector, which can also help identify them.

Bats eat beetles, flies and moths, including mosquitoes and midges. Some tropical species also pollinate plants. The most likely species to visit your garden are pipistrelles, which have a fast, jerky flight when hunting insects.

Bats don't make nests, but roost in a number of places, including trees and canal bridges. They use different roosts for different purposes, generally preferring warm roosts in summer and cold ones in winter.

HOW TO ATTRACT THEM: grow deciduous trees where insects can gather, dig a pond and grow plenty of plants for pollinators.

7. SQUIRREL

You may have the native red, *Sciurus vulgaris*, or the introduced grey, *Sciurus carolinensis*, in your garden. Both have similar habits, but the grey has displaced the red over much of the British Isles and parts of Italy.

The grey is native to North America and carries squirrel pox, which can be fatal to reds. Silvery grey with a large fluffy tail, it's bigger than the red, which is reddish-brown with a white belly, bushy tail and furry ears. Both eat tree seeds, flower buds and bulbs, shoots and fungi, but the grey is better at finding food.

Squirrel nests (dreys) are a messy ball of twigs made in holes in trees or where branches fork.

Breeding starts in late winter and females have up to two litters of around four kittens each year.

HOW TO ATTRACT THEM: feed reds to help them breed successfully, see p. 38 for details.

8. MOLE, *Talpa europaea*

The mole is about the same size as the hedgehog, with short, black velvety fur. It has squinty little eyes, a whiskery pink snout and giant spade-like hands. It spends almost all of its life underground. Mostly solitary, adults meet up in spring to mate, and litters contain three or four young.

Moles tend not to be loved by gardeners as they can cause havoc to vegetable plots and ornamental displays. But they can also be beneficial to the gardener: as well as earthworms, they eat cockchafer grubs and even carrot fly. Their tunnels also help to aerate and breakdown compacted soils.

They're present over most of Europe with the noticeable exception of Ireland, and are unlikely to visit gardens in urban areas.

HOW TO ATTRACT THEM: perhaps just tolerate them, rather than attract them. Grit your teeth and use the soil from molehills to sow seeds.

9. WEASEL/STOAT, *Mustela nivalis / Mustela erminea*

They're common and widespread in Europe, though the weasel is absent from Ireland. The stoat is larger than the weasel and has a longer tail with a black tip. They mainly eat mice and voles, but stoats take larger prey, such as rabbits.

Males and females establish separate territories, making a series of dens from the former nests of prey, which may be lined with the fur of the previous tenant. Mating takes place in late spring and early summer, but pregnancy is delayed in stoats until the following spring. Litters of up to twelve stoat kits and six weasels are born. After twelve weeks, the kits are ready to face the world on their own.

HOW TO ATTRACT THEM: if you live in a rural area, ensure your garden has a good supply of their favourite food: voles, rabbits, birds and eggs.

10. RABBIT, *Oryctolagus cuniculus*

Native to the Mediterranean, the rabbit is now a valuable part of our fauna and many species, including badgers, buzzards, weasels and stoats, rely on it for food. They're rarely welcome in gardens, as they eat fruit and vegetables and strip bark from young trees.

The rabbit has brown fur, a pale belly and long ears, and lives in an underground network of burrows and bolt-holes, known as a warren. Breeding takes place in spring and summer; the female builds a nest from grass, which she lines with soft fur from her belly, and gives birth to litters of up to seven kittens.

HOW TO ATTRACT THEM: it's probably not a great idea to encourage rabbits, but if they're already in your garden, arm yourself with some tree guards and a fruit and vegetable cage (60cm high and buried 5cm under the soil) and try to learn to live with them.

Right: If rabbits only stuck to grass, they'd be much more popular with gardeners.
Opposite: Note the dry, warty skin of this toad which enables it to spend long periods of time away from water.

AMPHIBIANS AND REPTILES

Amphibians and reptiles are gorgeous looking things, like creatures from a forgotten time. Many gardens are home to common frogs, toads and smooth newts, but you may also encourage slow worms, common lizards and even grass snakes to visit, depending on where you live.

Identifying them can be tricky, at first. Frogs are often mistaken for toads, smooth and palmate newts look virtually identical, and slow worms are often mistaken for snakes. But don't let this put you off! With a little practice, even the complete beginner can soon tell a common lizard from a smooth newt, a slow worm from a grass snake and a frog from a toad.

LOOK OUT FOR: mating frogs, toads and newts in spring, and grass snakes and common lizards basking in open sunshine.

Ten things to do for amphibians and reptiles

1. Dig a pond with gentle sloping sides and a deeper area if you have room, and plenty of aquatic plants
2. Create a large, open compost heap
3. Make a log pile
4. Let an area of grass go long, particularly around your pond
5. Build a dry stone wall
6. Create dense areas of vegetation in your borders
7. Sweep fallen leaves under your hedge or in a purpose-built wire cage
8. Avoid killing slugs and snails
9. Create basking areas
10. Make a hibernaculum (see p. 10 for details)

1. COMMON FROG, *Rana temporaria* * *Common and widespread*

No garden should be without the common frog, with its big eyes, shiny wet skin and appetite for slugs and snails.

Males tend to be smaller than females, especially when females develop spawn. In spring, males develop a single vocal sac, which looks like a large, double chin, and they can also take on a bluish tinge.

Fertilisation is external. Males grasp tightly on to females and spawn is laid in clumps. Tadpoles start off by eating algae, before developing a taste for the occasional bit of dead animal when their legs start to grow. Most froglets have left the pond by late summer, but won't be sexually active for two to three years.

In autumn, juvenile and female frogs overwinter in ditches and log and leaf piles, while many males head to the muddy bottom of ponds.

HOW TO ATTRACT THEM: dig a pond and make a log pile.

Breeding takes place throughout spring, with males appearing to 'dance' on the bottom of the pond. When a male has convinced a female to mate with him, he leaves his sperm in a packet called a spermatophore at the bottom of the pond, and she picks it up and fertilises herself internally. She then lays eggs, individually wrapping them in the leaves of plants such as water forget-me-not.

Newt larvae have external feathery gills behind their head. They leave the pond in late summer, when they're called newtlets or 'efts'. They spend winter sheltering under rocks or logs, or in compost heaps.

HOW TO ATTRACT THEM: grow pond plants such as water forget-me-not, and make piles of stones, leaf litter and logs for them to take shelter.

2. SMOOTH NEWT, *Lissotriton vulgaris* Common and widespread*
Brown with a spotty yellow-orange belly; only the male smooth newt develops a wavy crest during breeding season.

3. COMMON TOAD, *Bufo bufo* Common and widespread except for Ireland and northern Scandinavia*
The common toad has a round face and brown warty skin, which allows it to go for long periods away from

Opposite: A rare glimpse of a smooth newt as it exits a pond. **Top:** Common frogs can be identified by their pointed nose, shiny wet skin and black marks around the eyes. **Left:** A smooth newt looks for shelter on land. **Above:** The warty skin and more rounded appearance of toads identifies.

water. It also has a swollen poison gland behind each eye, making it slightly poisonous. It eats snails, slugs, ants, beetles and spiders.

Adults are known for returning to the pond they were born in, and make annual pilgrimages to ancestral mating grounds in spring. But this doesn't mean they won't use your garden pond. In every local population there are always a few that break away and try something new.

Mating is similar to that of frogs, usually taking place a couple of weeks later. Spawn is laid in strings and wrapped around submerged plant stems. Toadlets and adults spend the winter buried in mud, under compost heaps or amongst dead wood.

HOW TO ATTRACT THEM: dig a large, deep pond and make log and leaf piles.

4. SLOW WORM, *Anguis fragilis* Common and widespread except for Ireland, southern Spain and northern Scandinavia.*
The slow worm is commonly mistaken for a snake, but is actually a legless lizard. Unlike snakes, it has eyelids, and it can shed its tail to escape predators. Brown, shiny and almost iridescent, slow worms often gather in a large group, resembling a big clump of spaghetti drizzled with olive oil.

Males have a greyish tint and females have dark sides. Babies are thin with gold or silver sides. They mainly eat slugs (snails, woodlice, earthworms and insects are also taken). Compost bins provide the perfect, warm conditions, but they also take refuge under log piles and strips of corrugated iron laid in a sunny, secluded spot.

Breeding takes place in late spring. Females incubate their eggs internally and give birth to around eight live young in late summer.

HOW TO ATTRACT THEM: provide access to your compost bin and make a log pile.

A slow worm retreats to the safety of long grass.

A grass snake travels through long grass.

5. GRASS SNAKE, *Natrix natrix* Common and widespread except for Ireland and northern Scandinavia*
Non-venomous, the worst a grass snake can do to you is release a foul smelling liquid, or musk, if you pick it up (it's not actually that foul smelling – rather like wild garlic). It has a distinctive yellow collar around the neck, a scaly, olive-green body and a beautiful black forked tongue.

Females tend to be longer than males (they can grow to 1.2m, while males only reach 1m), although most you see will be quite small. Breeding takes place in late spring and eggs are laid in in early summer in compost heaps and other warm piles of vegetation. They overwinter in compost heaps, log piles and beneath tree roots. Babies eat tadpoles and juvenile amphibians, moving on to adult frogs, toads, newts and occasionally goldfish as they mature.

HOW TO ATTRACT THEM: dig a pond, and make a large, open compost heap for them to breed in.

6. COMMON LIZARD, *Zootoca vivipara* Common and widespread*
Small and fast-moving, the common lizard is more likely to turn up in rural gardens. It has scaly, chequered skin, and individuals range in colour from dark green to grey-brown. The young are much darker than the adults – some are almost black. It eats flies, grasshoppers, ants and spiders, and can lose its tail to escape from predators.

Breeding takes place in April and May. The eggs are incubated internally and up to eleven young are born in July.

You may spot several at a time, basking on wood and stone in spring and autumn. Individuals choose favourite sites which they regularly return to. They disappear in late autumn, hibernating in crevices and abandoned burrows.

HOW TO ATTRACT THEM: make a log pile in a sunny spot, which they will use for basking and hibernating, and let a patch of grass grow long so they can hunt for prey.

9. GREAT CRESTED NEWT, *Triturus cristatus* Common and widespread, but declining*
This declining newt is unlikely to visit your garden unless you have suitable habitat nearby. The large adults have almost black warty skin with a spotted yellow-orange belly, and males develop a jagged crest and white tail stripe during breeding season.

Adults tend to live on land, though some may stay in ponds to feed after breeding. They prefer larger ponds and ditches, but may visit smaller garden ponds. They have an elaborate courtship routine in which males drive pheromones towards females with their tails. Females lay eggs in the leaves of pond plants. Newtlets, or efts, emerge from ponds between August and October, and hibernation takes place on land.

HOW TO ATTRACT THEM: tell someone from your local Amphibian and Reptile Group if you have them in your garden. Great crested newts are protected by UK and European law, so you need a licence to disturb them.

INSECTS – BEES AND WASPS

Nearly all gardens have a range of bees passing through, from fluffy fat bumbles to little zippy things that never stay still for long enough for you to see what they are. Gardens are fantastic resources for bees, especially in early spring and late autumn, when wild sources of nectar and pollen can be in short supply. Most bees are harmless, although honeybees can be aggressive if they perceive a threat to their colony. Bumblebees and solitary bees rarely, if ever, sting.

Wasps, too, are well catered for in our gardens. As well as social wasps, which include the much-maligned common wasp, *Vespula vulgaris*, there are lesser known parasitic species. These live solitary lives, laying eggs in other insects and their larvae. All wasps are predatory and do a great job of controlling caterpillars and aphids. Most of them go unnoticed and, like bees, rarely sting. In late summer, common wasp workers can become aggressive, as well as irritate during summer picnics.

Above: A solitary bee gorges on flowering currant in spring.
Opposite: A common carder bumblebee feeds on knapweed.

LOOK OUT FOR:

Bumblebees – furry and often stripy. Most have black and yellow stripes with a white tail, but some have a gingery or mostly black coat. Many can be identified by the colour of their tails. They live in colonies in holes in the ground, tussocky grass and compost bins. Workers are female and can be identified by the little baskets of pollen they carry on their hind legs. Males often have a bit of facial hair, or a 'moustache'.

Lifecycle – colonies are annual. The large queen emerges from hibernation in spring and starts a nest. She then spends her time laying eggs while her workers gather nectar and pollen for the grubs. In summer, she produces males and daughter queens, which mate, before the males die and the daughter queens find somewhere to hibernate, ready to start a new nest in spring. The original queen and her workers also die.

Honeybees – smaller and thinner than bumblebees, with little or no hair on the abdomen. They range in colour from orange to almost black and tend to live in large hives owned by beekeepers, but they occasionally start a new colony on their own – often in a tree.

Lifecycle – social, like bumblebees, but colonies can reach up to 40,000 workers and last for years. In spring, the original queen and thousands of workers may 'swarm' to start a new colony elsewhere, and daughter queens may also set off with a few hundred workers to establish colonies of their own. Honeybees are at their most docile when swarming, and are usually collected by beekeepers.

Solitary bees – can look like anything from bumblebees and honeybees, to wasps. If you have a

A large buff-tailed queen replenishes her reserves on perennial wallflower.

solitary bee box, you may attract red mason bees or leafcutter bees, and look out for hairy-footed flower bees in early spring.

Lifecycle – they don't live in colonies, but lay eggs in individual cells, which they leave with a parcel of pollen and nectar for the emerging grub to eat. Some burrow in the ground, others lay eggs in hollow plant stems or even holes in walls. Once grown, the grubs pupate into adults and overwinter in the nest, before emerging at exactly the right time the following year, to mate and start the whole process all over again. Many solitary bees are loyal to a particular nesting site, so the ancestors of the bees nesting in your wall, lawn or borders, may have been doing so for years.

Wasps – tend to have no body hair and a thin waist. Most social wasps, including hornets, have yellow and black or brown striped bodies. Parasitic wasps range in colour and often have an extremely long ovipositor (egg-laying organ).

Lifecycle – most are social and make intricate nests from chewed wood, which they rasp from untreated fence posts, trees and even garden furniture. Nests can house up to 20,000 workers. Parasitic wasps lay eggs in other insects.

Ten things to do for bees and wasps
1. Grow a wide range of flowering plants from March to November
2. Let an area of grass grow long but also keep areas short – especially if solitary bees are already nesting there
3. Provide access to your compost heap
4. Make log, stick and leaf piles
5. Make a solitary bee hotel
6. Leave patches of bare earth for solitary bees
7. Provide a source of water (such as a bird bath with a few stones in) for honeybees
8. Grow a variety of caterpillar foodplants, for wasps
9. Make a pile of grass clippings
10. Provide a source of untreated wood, such as a fence post or bird box, for social wasps

1. BUFF-TAILED BUMBLEBEE, *Bombus terrestris*
This is a large, widespread and robust bumblebee. The enormous queens are often the first to emerge in spring, sometimes as early as February. A very small number may even establish winter colonies and forage on winter-flowering shrubs such as mahonia and daphne. Nests are usually made underground.

Mostly black with a dark yellow band on the thorax and one on the abdomen, only the queen has an obvious buff-coloured tail (this can occasionally be orange-red). The short-tongued workers visit almost any type of flower they can access nectar and pollen, and may even pierce holes in flowers with long flower tubes to access nectar they would otherwise be unable to reach (if you've ever seen holes in the top of your broad bean flower, that's why). Queens may also drink aphid honeydew.

HOW TO ATTRACT THEM: grow winter flowering plants and provide access to your compost bin.

2. RED-TAILED BUMBLEBEE, *Bombus lapidarius*

Velvet black with an orange-red tail, the red-tailed bumblebee is gorgeous. Queens can be quite large, but the size or workers varies. Nests are established in spring. Males can be told from workers by a thin, lemon-yellow band on the thorax and a yellow 'moustache'. Workers have a short tongue and visit a wide range of flowers, but seem to have a preference for yellow ones, including bird's foot trefoil.

Like the buff-tailed bumblebee, the red-tailed may nest underground in old mouse holes, but may also nest in wall cavities (I once found a nest in an old duvet that had been slung out).

HOW TO ATTRACT THEM: grow yellow flowers, especially bird's foot trefoil. They will also be attracted to a mini 'meadow' of cornfield annuals such as cornflowers.

3. COMMON CARDER BUMBLEBEE, *Bombus pascuorum*

Little and ginger, the common carder typically nests in tussocky grass but will also use compost bins and piles of grass clippings. The bees collect moss and 'card' it together to cover the nest. Workers vary in size and can be so small they resemble honeybees. They have a medium to long tongue, so feed on plants with long flower tubes like honeysuckle,

foxgloves and white deadnettle. All of this bobbing in and out of flowers can make the workers lose a lot of hair, and you may see one with a triangular-shaped bald patch on its thorax. They're also susceptible to being bleached by the sun, so can look quite raggedy by autumn. Common carder nests seem to go on and on – in milder areas it's not unusual to find workers still on the wing in November.

HOW TO ATTRACT THEM: leave a patch of grass to grow long and tussocky. Grow flowers with long flower tubes, like honeysuckle and foxgloves.

4. CUCKOO BUMBLEBEES

Rather than build a colony of their own, cuckoos take over the nests of other bumblebees. There are no queens or workers – just males and females. Most species have specific hosts, which they have evolved to resemble. They emerge from hibernation much later than their hosts, giving the host queen time to get a nest established.

Unlike bumblebee queens and workers, cuckoos have no pollen baskets, because they only need to feed themselves. They're larger and less hairy than bumblebees, and have a very pointed abdomen tip. Some have smoky wings.

Only the female takes over a nest. On finding a nest she may then wait outside for a few days to take on its scent in order to enter unnoticed. She then enters, kills the queen and lays her own eggs, which the existing workers feed.

HOW TO ATTRACT THEM: ensure you have the perfect nesting conditions for bumblebees.

5. HONEYBEE, *Apis mellifera*

The honeybee is small and slender. It has less body hair than bumblebees – typically a hairy thorax, with fewer hairs on the abdomen. Workers can vary in colour, with some being quite orange and others almost black. They're generalist feeders with a short tongue, so can visit a range of open, single flowers. Like bumblebees, honeybee workers collect pollen in 'baskets' on their hind legs, and drink nectar. When they return to the colony they regurgitate the nectar and comb the pollen off their legs. This is mixed together and made into honey, which is used to feed the grubs. (Bumblebee 'honey' is more watery than the stuff produced by honeybees. This is because a team of workers flap their wings to evaporate excess water from the mixture, whereas bumblebees don't.)

HOW TO ATTRACT THEM: grow a variety of plants with nectar- and pollen-rich flowers.

Honeybee.

6. LEAFCUTTER BEE, *Megachile*

Solitary, but prone to nesting communally, leafcutters are easy to spot due to their habit of cutting semi-circular pieces out of rose and wisteria leaves and carrying them to their nests. They also have a rather comical tendency to lift up their abdomen when feeding. There are several species, which superficially look similar looking to honeybees, but they have a patch of orange hairs on the base of their abdomen (called scopa), on which they collect pollen.

They nest in hollow plant stems and dead wood, and readily use solitary bee boxes. Compared to honey and bumblebees, leafcutters are only on the wing for a relatively short time, typically between June and August.

HOW TO ATTRACT THEM: make a solitary bee box (see p. 17 for details), and grow roses and wisterias.

7. RED MASON BEE, *Osmia rufa*

This solitary bee nests in old wood and hollow plant stems, even walls (although no damage is done) and readily uses bee boxes. Mason bees get their name from their habit of sealing their nests with mud. The red mason bee is said to be one of the most efficient pollinators of spring fruit trees, including apples, plums and cherries.

Covered in gingery red hairs, adults emerge from March onwards, and are normally on the wing until about June. Males are smaller than females and sport a little tuft of white hair on the face. They mate, and the female lays eggs near where she was born – she may even return to the same solitary bee box.

HOW TO ATTRACT THEM: make a solitary bee box (see p. 17 for details), and leave a dish of mud out in spring, in case of dry weather.

8. NOMADA BEES, *Nomada*

If you have ground-nesting solitary bees in your garden, take a closer look at the nest burrows and you may see small, wasp-like bees flying around, too. These are beautiful Nomada bees, which are cleptoparasites (food stealers) of solitary bees in the *Andrena* genus.

Female Nomada bees lay their eggs in the cells created by the host bee for their own young. The host makes a cell, into which she leaves a parcel of pollen and nectar and lays an egg, and the Nomada bee comes along and also lays an egg. This hatches into a grub, which eats the other grub, pollen and nectar, and emerges the following spring to start the process all over again.

HOW TO ATTRACT THEM: create the perfect conditions for ground-nesting solitary bees, including bare patches of sandy soil and lawns.

Nomada bee.

9. COMMON WASP, *Vespula vulgaris*

The common wasp is virtually hairless, and is easily recognised by its bright yellow and black body and anchor-shaped facial mark. Like bumblebees, it lives in annual colonies, but workers feed caterpillars and other insects to the young rather than pollen and nectar, in return for a sugary substance secreted by the grubs. They only become annoying in late summer, when the nest breaks down and there are no longer any grubs to feed.

Without the sugary returns from the young, workers look to fruit trees, jam sandwiches and fizzy drinks for a sugary fix. They can become drunk on the alcohol in fermenting fruit, which makes them clumsy, aggressive, and more likely to sting. This usually lasts for a couple of weeks before they die. Only mated queens hibernate, ready to start a new generation of pest controllers next year.

HOW TO ATTRACT THEM: if you can't love them, do try to tolerate them.

10. PARASITIC WASPS

Many wasps are solitary and parasitic, rather than living in large colonies. The most noticeable in our gardens are the ichneumons. Females often have incredibly long ovipositors, which may be mistaken for a terrifying sting. Eggs are laid in, on or next to eggs, larvae, pupae or adults of other insects or spiders, and the emerging grub eats its host.

Some species, such as the giant ichneumon, *Rhyssa persuasoria*, locate prey deep within rotting wood. The female detects her prey by scent or from vibrations in the wood, and uses her long ovipositor to bore down and lay an egg next to her victim. The egg hatches and the grub eats its host, before overwintering and pupating in spring.

HOW TO ATTRACT THEM: grow plenty of plants, make a log pile and tolerate caterpillars.

BUTTERFLIES AND MOTHS

There's something about watching a beautiful butterfly visiting a beautiful flower that makes everything seem all right with the world. Who can resist the charms of the peacock, or fail to be enchanted by the common blue? Sadly, of the whopping 440 European species of butterfly, far less will visit gardens, unless you live near a particularly good habitat. On top of that, few can be encouraged to breed in our gardens, but the good thing is that many will stop for lunch.

Moths will readily breed in gardens although many are night flyers, so often go unnoticed. They're often seen as the ugly cousins of butterflies, but they can be just as beautiful. They're also fascinating. Did you know that some have developed ears so they can hear when bats are coming after them?

LOOK OUT FOR:

Butterflies – often brightly coloured, but some are mostly white and others brown. They're categorised into six families: skippers, swallowtails, whites, nymphalids (the most common garden species), browns, blues coppers and hairstreaks, and finally, metalmarks (of which there's only one in Europe – the Duke of Burgundy).

Lifecycle – adults emerge in spring or summer, mate, lay eggs and then die. Depending on the species, a second or even third generation may emerge later in the year, which will either mate or build up fat reserves to hibernate or migrate back to southern Europe. Most species spend winter as a caterpillar or pupa.

Moths – many are brown and hard to identify, but some are as colourful as butterflies, especially day-flying species. Night-flying adults may be disturbed while gardening – they rest on tree bark, sheds and outhouses. They're far more numerous than butterflies, there are thirteen families of larger moths, not to mention all the micro species. Common families include the noctuids, geometrids, hawk-moths and tigers.

Lifecycle – similar to butterflies. While most emerge in spring and summer, lots don't appear until autumn and some, such as the December moth, are active in mid-winter. Moths are less fussy than butterflies, with most feeding on a wide range of plants.

Ten things to do for butterflies and moths

1. Grow caterpillar foodplants, including nettles, buckthorn, hops and lady's smock
2. Grow a variety of nectar-rich plants from March to November, planting them in large, easy-to-find groups
3. Leave windfall apples in autumn
4. Plant native deciduous trees and shrubs
5. Leave a patch of grass to grow long, or cultivate a meadow
6. Plant a hedge and avoid trimming it every year (then cut it in late winter)
7. Use rocks or large stones to create basking areas in full sunshine
8. Avoid clearing ornamental borders in autumn
9. Tolerate a few 'weeds' such as bramble, plantains, dandelions and nettles
10. Avoid cutting down plants in autumn, which might be sheltering caterpillars or harbouring pupae

1. ORANGE-TIP, *Anthocharis cardamines*

The orange-tip is mostly white, with green mottling to the undersides of its wings. Only the male has orange wing tips, the tips of the female's wings are black. Adults are mostly seen in late spring to early summer, flying along hedgerows, the edges of woodland and gardens.

In spring, the female lays single bright orange eggs on the flower buds of crucifers, including hedge mustard (*Alliaria petiolata*), lady's smock (*Cardamine pratensis*), honesty (*Lunaria annua*) and dame's violet (*Hesperis matronalis*). The small, green and white caterpillars feed on the flowers and developing seedpods, before pupating and overwintering as a chrysalis on or near the foodplant. New adults finally emerge the following spring.

HOW TO ATTRACT THEM: grow nectar-rich, spring flowering plants, especially lady's smock, which orange-tips also use to lay eggs.

2. RED ADMIRAL, *Vanessa atalanta*

The red admiral has dark brown/black wings with red bands and white spots near the tips. Adults migrate northwards from North Africa and the Mediterranean each year. They arrive in spring, mate and lay eggs, with their offspring emerging in summer. Second generation adults feed from plants such as buddleia and ivy, to build up reserves for the long flight south. They also drink the juice from blackberries and windfall fruit. In milder areas, some now overwinter rather than fly south in autumn.

The red admiral breeds on nettles. Caterpillars fold the leaves together to make a tent to shelter them from predators, and can be black, greenish-brown or pale yellow, depending on their size.

HOW TO ATTRACT THEM: if you don't have room for a large patch of nettles growing in full sun, grow plenty of late-flowering plants such as buddleia, sedums and Michaelmas daisies

3. SPECKLED WOOD BUTTERFLY, *Pararge aegeria*

Rich chocolate-brown with creamy white patches, the speckled wood is typically found in woodland, but is now increasingly seen in gardens. Adults usually drink honeydew secreted by aphids high up in the trees, but switch to nectar in early spring and late summer, when aphids can be in short supply.

Adults emerge in spring and breed in grass, including false brome (*Brachypodium sylvaticumi*), cock's-foot (*Dactylis glomerata*) and common couch (*Elytrigia repens*). There are usually at least two broods, so you may still see them on the wing in September. They hibernate in grass, either as a bright green caterpillar, or chrysalis.

HOW TO ATTRACT THEM: let an area of grass grow long and tussocky and provide early and late sources of nectar.

4. SMALL TORTOISESHELL, *Aglais urticae*

With its bright orange and black wings edged with a row of delicate blue dots, the small tortoiseshell is easy to identify, though it may be confused with the less common (and probably extinct in Britain) large tortoiseshell.

Adults hibernate in sheds and outhouses, emerging in spring to mate, and lay eggs on large clumps of nettles. Their caterpillars build communal webs to shelter from predators, and emerge as adults in summer. Second generation adults are often found feeding on buddleia bushes.

Generally widespread and common, populations in the south-east of the UK have recently suffered huge declines, in part due to the arrival of a parasitic fly, *Sturmia bella*, from mainland Europe.

HOW TO ATTRACT THEM: if you don't have room for a large patch of nettles growing in full sun, grow plenty of late-flowering plants such as buddleia, sedums and Michaelmas daisies.

5. COMMA BUTTERFLY, *Polygonia c-album*

The comma is a master of disguise. Its orangey-brown raggedy wings resemble fallen leaves when resting, and its brown and white caterpillars look a bit like bird droppings. But it's the white, comma-shaped mark on the undersides of the wings that gives it its name.

Adults emerge from hibernation in spring, mate and lay eggs on stinging nettles, but they're less fussy than most, so will also breed on hops, currants, elms and willows. (In some parts of Europe they use sallow and birch.) The second generation appears in summer and may go on to produce a third generation in milder areas. Adults fatten themselves up on a variety of nectar-rich flowers and ripe fruit, before hibernating.

HOW TO ATTRACT THEM: encourage adults to breed by growing hops, currants (including gooseberry) or elms.

Top: A small tortoiseshell takes nectar from heather flowers. **Left:** A peacock butterfly visits on echinacea flower. **Right:** A comma basks in the autumn sunshine.

6. SWALLOWTAIL, *Papilio machaon* Common and widespread, except for Britain*

This large butterfly is common and widespread over much of Europe, but rare in Britain, where it has evolved into a smaller and less brightly coloured subspecies, *britannicus*.

The British swallowtail lives exclusively in the Norfolk broads and breeds exclusively on milk parsley (*Peucedanum palustre*). By contrast, European swallowtails are common garden visitors and lay eggs on a variety of umbellifers, including fennel and carrots – in some instances, they're considered pests.

Adults fly in late spring and summer. British swallowtails have just one brood, but elsewhere they have two. Initially, caterpillars are black, marked with a band of white, but eventually become bright green with narrow black bands and orange spots. Pupae are green or light brown with a dark stripe. Like all butterflies in the Papilionidae family, they keep their wings fluttering while feeding.

HOW TO ATTRACT THEM: grow a range of nectar-rich flowers for adults.

7. RUBY TIGER MOTH, *Phragmatobia fuliginosa*

This is a handsome moth, with a red body, velvety brown forewings and pinkish hindwings (though colouring can vary, with northern moths having darker wings). It can be found in a variety of habitats including gardens, and will also fly during the day, particularly in sunshine.

In the south, adults fly and breed from April to June and again from August to September, but in the north there is just one brood, typically in June. Their gorgeous 'woolly bear' caterpillars feed on a number of plants including ragworts, plantains, heathers, dock, dandelion, spindle and broom. They overwinter as caterpillars in leaf litter and other debris.

HOW TO ATTRACT THEM: tolerate a few weeds to grow as caterpillar foodplants and make leaf piles for overwintering caterpillars.

Left: A red admiral rests on a bramble leaf.
Right: A mint moth rests on catmint foliage.

8. SILVER Y MOTH, *Autographa gamma*

Named after the letter y that appears to be painted on each forewing in silvery gold, this migrant moth is easy to identify. It's resident in southern Europe, parts of Asia and North Africa, and migrates north in spring, sometimes reaching as far as Finland and the Arctic Circle. In some years adults can arrive in huge numbers. They normally appear in May and have usually flown south by the first frosts.

Adults fly during the day and night, regularly visiting gardens to drink from nectar-rich flowers. Several generations occur each year, with the green caterpillars eating a range of plants including garden peas, cabbages, clovers and stinging nettles.

HOW TO ATTRACT THEM: grow nectar-rich plants for the adults, and nettles and clover and their caterpillars. If you find any caterpillars on your pea plants, simply transfer to a patch of nettles or clover.

9. ELEPHANT HAWK-MOTH, *Deilelphila elpenor*

Named after the caterpillar's apparent resemblance to an elephant's trunk, this hawk-moth is one of the most exciting pollinators we can encourage into our gardens. All hawk-moths have spectacular caterpillars, with a spike, or horn on their 'tail'. The elephant hawk-moth's caterpillars are green or brown and have enormous eye-spots and a snout (like an elephant). They mainly feed on rosebay willowherb (*Epilobium angustifolium*), but also eat bedstraws (*Galium*) and garden fuchsias. At a whopping 7.5cm, caterpillars are often found on the ground in September, looking to burrow into a patch of soil to pupate for winter.

The bright pink and green adults emerge from May to July, visiting honeysuckle and other garden plants for nectar.

HOW TO ATTRACT THEM: tolerate a small patch of rosebay willowherb, on to which you can transfer caterpillars from your fuchsias.

10. ANGLE SHADES, *Phlogophora meticulosa*

The angle shades is named after its unusual angled shape. It's brownish in colour, with triangular pink and green markings in the centre of each wing. Adults emerge in spring and mainly fly at night. They're often found resting on fences or garden foliage during the day. There are at least two broods every year. Only the caterpillars overwinter, emerging in spring to pupate.

Some gardeners might not appreciate its caterpillar's habit of eating anything from aeoniums, chrysanthemums and dahlias to basil and pelargoniums. But don't forget that a large proportion of moth caterpillars are taken by birds and wasps, so they may not have much chance to damage your plants.

HOW TO ATTRACT THEM: learn to live with them – grow birch, red valerian, ivy and oak, on to which you can transfer any rogue caterpillars.

BEETLES

When it comes to garden wildlife, beetles are often overlooked. They're not nearly as popular as bees and butterflies; you don't find gardening articles entitled 'Save the beetle!' and few writers try to explain how endearing they are (except for the ladybird, which many people don't realise is a beetle). Perhaps it's because many live in compost bins or among leaf litter, that some of them only come out at night or that their grubs often look a bit like maggots (and can be garden pests). But beetles are just as interesting (and occasionally cute) as bees and butterflies. And many of them are also declining.

The beetle family is the largest group of insects in the world. There are large ones and small ones, shiny red ones and dull brown ones, some that eat our plants and some that eat other insects that eat our plants. They typically have a thick pair of forewings or wing cases, called elytra, which protect the more delicate hind wings used for flying. Others don't fly at all.

The crocodile-like larva of a ten-spot ladybird homes in on an aphid colony.

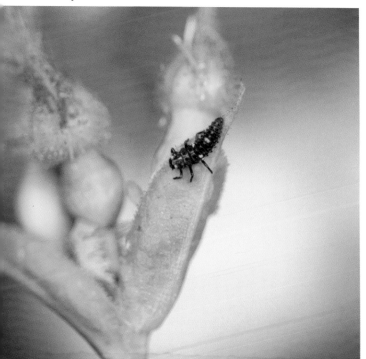

LOOK OUT FOR: You'll find beetles anywhere from your plants to your compost bin and log pile. The larvae often look like maggots – such as chafer grubs – but they can also look like baby crocodiles, like ladybird larvae.

Ten things to do for beetles

1. Leave dead wood on trees, where possible
2. Make a log pile (bury some of the logs in the ground if you can)
3. Sweep fallen leaves under your hedge or gather them in a bespoke wire cage
4. Mulch borders with leafmould
5. Leave an old tree stump to rot into itself
6. Create areas of densely planted vegetation
7. Plant an oak (if you have space)
8. Grow a patch of nettles for aphid-eating ladybirds
9. Allow mildew to develop on leaves, for mildew-eating ladybirds
10. Grow a range of flowering plants, including umbelliefers

1. RED SOLDIER BEETLE, *Rhagonycha fulva*

It's known as Weichkäfer (soft beetle) in Germany, but in the UK it's sometimes called the bonking beetle, for rather obvious reasons. If you have them in your garden you will nearly always find them mating on flowers.

There are lots of different type of soldier beetle, all with narrow bodies and long antennae. *Rhagonycha fulva* grows up to a centimetre in length and is yellow-red in colour, with black tips on the wing cases.

Adults fly in summer and feed on insects, which they hunt from flowers. After mating, the female lays her eggs in the soil and the brown larvae feed on small snails and insects. A year later, the larvae pupate and emerge as adult beetles, ready to go off in search of flowers to mate on.

HOW TO ATTRACT THEM: plant a mini meadow, with plenty of grasses and umbellifers such as hogweed and cow parsley.

2. WASP BEETLE, *Clytus arietis*

Black, with yellow bands and relatively short antennae, this long-horn beetle pretends to be a wasp to avoid being eaten by predators. It even mimics the common wasp's jerky movements and can emit a threatening buzz when disturbed. But it doesn't sting and is completely harmless.

Adults are thin and long-bodied, and fly from May to July. You might spot them scrambling over vegetation on sunny days. They feed on a variety of flowers for pollen and nectar, though females also eat small insects.

After mating, the female seeks out dead, rotting wood, including dead branches and even garden fence posts, to lay eggs. The larvae live and feed in this dead wood, before pupating and emerging as adults the following year.

HOW TO ATTRACT THEM: ensure there is plenty of dead wood in your garden, especially if it's still attached to trees.

3. VIOLET GROUND BEETLE, *Carabus violaceus*

Ground beetles are a must-have in gardens, for the simple reason that they eat snails and other garden pests. There are hundreds of different types, with the violet ground beetle being one of the easiest to identify. This is large (3cm long) and black with a metallic violet sheen to the edges of its wing cases and thorax. Adults hunt at night, hiding by day under logs or stones. They don't fly, but they're very fast runners.

As with other beetles in the *Carabus* genus, both adults and their larvae prey on slugs, snails, worms and insects. After mating, females lay their eggs in soil. The larvae start hunting as soon as they've hatched out of the egg.

HOW TO ATTRACT THEM: make a log pile and mulch your borders with leafmould.

4. ROVE BEETLES

Rove beetles are an enormous genus of beetles that you may find living in your compost bin. They're easy to tell apart from other beetles because their wing cases don't cover their abdomens, so they look a bit half-dressed. One of the most well recognised is the coach horse beetle, *Ocypus olens*, which is black and known for raising its abdomen like a scorpion when disturbed (it's harmless, but might give you a nip if handled).

Most prey on insects and other invertebrates, such as snails, worms and caterpillars. Some also eat slug and snail eggs, fungus gnat larvae and even aphids. The tiny eggs are laid in groups, often close to a potential food source. The larvae then feed for a couple of weeks before pupating in the soil.

HOW TO ATTRACT THEM: compost waste, make log piles and mulch your plants.

5. SEVEN-SPOT LADYBIRD, *Coccinella septempunctata*

Every gardener loves ladybirds, probably because they're pretty, slow-moving and eat a lot of aphids. There are many types, of which the seven-spot is the most common and easily recognised. It has red wing cases marked with seven black dots (three on either wing case and one spread over the junction of the two).

Adults emerge in spring, mate and the female lays eggs on plants infested with aphids. When the eggs

A seven-spot ladybird rests on a leaf.

A two-spot ladybird rests on a leaf.

hatch, the crocodile-like larvae hoover up the aphids, before attaching to a leaf and pupating into an orange and black pupa. The adult usually hatches out within a week. There's normally just one brood a year, with the second generation fattening up on aphids in preparation for hibernation.

HOW TO ATTRACT THEM: grow nettles to attract the nettle aphid early in the year.

6. TWO-SPOT LADYBIRD, *Adalia bipunctata*

The two-spot is smaller than the seven-spot and has a narrower body shape. It comes in many colour forms, the two commonest being red with one black spot on each wing case, or black with two red spots on each wing case. The spots can be variable, and can appear square-shaped or as splodges.

Since the arrival of the harlequin ladybird to Europe, populations of two-spots have suffered. Harlequins were first recorded in Belgium in 2001 and Britain in 2004. Since then, two-spot ladybirds

have declined by 30 per cent in Belgium and 44 per cent in Britain. Harlequins and two-spots are tree-dwelling aphid eaters, and it's thought that the harlequin – which is bigger, stronger and breeds more often – outcompetes the two-spots, as well as eating them.

HOW TO ATTRACT THEM: avoid killing aphids and grow nettles.

7. HARLEQUIN LADYBIRD, *Harmonia axyridis*

The harlequin is an alien invader of the worst kind. Originally from Asia but used as biological pest control in the United States and Europe, it's been bred to be bigger, stronger, faster and hungrier than its Asian ancestors. It was only a matter of time before it spread across Europe and over the Channel.

It is difficult to tell apart from native species, though it tends to be bigger and has more of a domed body shape. You're likely to find one of three colour

A harlequin rests on a leaf.

Revealing its appetite for aphids, this harlequin makes light work of a greenfly.

forms in your garden: red or orange with black spots (succinea); black with four red spots (spectabilis); and black with two red spots (conspicua).

The only thing it's got going for it is its appetite for aphids, but it also eats moth eggs, lacewings and other native ladybirds.

HOW TO ATTRACT THEM: avoid killing them as you may kill a native ladybird by mistake.

8. COMMON COCKCHAFER, *Melolontha melolontha*
Also known as the May bug because it flies in May, the common cockchafer is large, brown and noisy. It has a black thorax, rusty brown wing cases, brown legs and wonderful feathery antennae.

Cockchafers used to be common, but because their larvae eat plant roots, they became victims of pesticide campaigns across Europe and were almost wiped out in the 1970s. Numbers are now recovering but they're nowhere near as common as they used to be.

Adults appear in May and live for up to seven weeks, feeding on flowers and leaves. During that time they mate and the female lays eggs in the soil. The larvae feed on plant roots for several years, before eventually pupating one autumn. The cockchafer then overwinters as an adult, only climbing to the surface in spring.

HOW TO ATTRACT THEM: plant shrubs and trees, which they sometimes fly around in groups.

FLIES

For many people, the word 'fly' conjures up images of irritating houseflies, or rotting carrion, faeces and maggots. Then there are the mosquitoes, midges and horse flies. Surely they're not worthy of being welcomed into the garden?

And yet flies are an invaluable source of food for countless other species. Swifts, swallows, house martins and a multitude of other birds eat flies, as do bats, dragonflies and amphibians. Without flies, we wouldn't have these other species, and some are already declining due to a general lack of insects, i.e., flies!

Flies are also valuable in their own right. Many have the incredibly important job of helping to break down decaying matter, while others, such as hoverflies, eat aphids.

LOOK OUT FOR:

Hoverflies – often look like a stinging insect to avoid detection. Adults eat nectar and pollen but the larvae eat aphids or damp, organic matter.

Lifecycle – eggs are laid in spring and summer, either on plants infested by aphids or in rot holes or compost heaps. Many species are multi-brooded. Most hoverflies overwinter as larvae, only pupating when temperatures increase in spring.

Bee-flies – furry, like bumblebees, but with a large, rigid proboscis and a darting, jerky flight. Adults drink nectar but the larvae eat the detritus in solitary bee and wasp nests.

Lifecycle – There are several species, all of which lay eggs in the nests of solitary bees and wasps.

Ten things to do for flies

1. Grow a variety of flowering plants, particularly umbellifers
2. Dig a pond
3. Compost waste
4. Leave an old tree stump standing
5. Let an area of grass grow long
6. Tolerate aphids
7. Recreate a rot hole by steeping leaves in water
8. Make a pile of grass clippings
9. Create overwintering sites by mulching borders and making piles of leaves
10. Grow a variety of caterpillar foodplants, for parasitic flies

1. LARGE BEE-FLY, *Bombylius major*

If you see a large, ginger-brown 'bee' with an enormous proboscis visiting your primroses or grape hyacinths, it's bound to be the large bee-fly. This is not a bee, but a bee mimic, which hums and hovers and darts quickly around spring flowers. On closer inspection you can tell it's a fly because it has only one pair of wings (bees have two). The wings are dark and the body is brown and furry, and it has a protruding rigid proboscis.

After mating, the female flicks her eggs into the underground nests of solitary bees and wasps and the larvae feed on the stores of food and grubs inside. She may also lay eggs on flowers visited by solitary bees and wasps, and the larvae hitch a ride on the bodies of unsuspecting victims.

HOW TO ATTRACT THEM: grow primroses, grape hyacinths, violet and bugle.

2. HOVERFLY, *Volucella bombylans*

This hoverfly is also a bee mimic, part of a genus of large, dramatic-looking hoverflies. To the untrained eye, *Volucella bombylans* looks similar to a bumblebee, but on closer inspection it has one pair of (dark) wings.

There are several subspecies, which mimic different bumblebees. *Volucella bombylans var. Bombylans* has an orange tail, and so mimics the red-tailed bumblebee, while *Volucella bombylans var. plumata* has a white tail, mimicking white-tailed bumblebees.

Adults are found in gardens (as well as along hedgerows, in urban waste ground and woodland margins) from May until September. They feed on nectar and pollen and the larvae feed on the debris (and occasionally the larvae) of bumblebee and social wasp nests. Adults are often seen sunning themselves on leaves or fence posts.

HOW TO ATTRACT THEM: grow a good range of flowering plants in spring and summer.

3. HOVERFLY, *Myathropa florea*

This beautiful creature is one of a number of hoverflies in the *Eristalis* genus, which start their lives as slightly less appealing rat-tailed maggots. The bright yellow and black-striped adults fly from May to October and feed on a variety of garden umbellifers. By contrast, their larvae eat bacteria and decaying organic matter in stagnant, waterlogged detritus such as shallow rot holes in tree stumps, compost heaps and even drains. But don't let this put you off. The 'rat tail' is merely a breathing tube which the larva uses as a snorkel, allowing it to breath under water.

HOW TO ATTRACT THEM: grow a range of umbellifers, including cow parsley and Bishop's flower, *Ammi majus*, and leave tree stumps to rot. If you're really keen, you could create your own 'rot hole' in a bucket – just add water and leaves.

The squared-off end indicated this is a male.

4. CRANE FLY, *Tipula paludosa*

This is one of many species of crane fly you'll find dancing around your lawn in summer and autumn. The long-legged spider-like flies are also known as daddy-long-legs and are often cursed by gardeners for their 'leatherjacket' larvae, which eat plant roots and can, in large numbers, cause unsightly brown patches in lawns.

Tipula paludosa has a slender, grey-brown body and long legs. Males have a swollen and square-ended abdomen, while the females have a pointed end, used to lay eggs in the soil.

The larvae form an important food source for birds. It's even been suggested that the decline of starlings is the result of pesticide use, which has reduced numbers of crane flies in agricultural areas. So, if you can tolerate them in your garden, you could well help to prevent further starling declines.

HOW TO ATTRACT THEM: keep your lawn fairly short.

5. MARMALADE HOVERFLY, *Episyrphus balteatus*

The marmalade hoverfly is a small, tiger-striped insect, which feeds on pollen and nectar from a variety of garden flowers. Males establish territories which they guard religiously, patiently waiting for females to fly past. After mating, females lay eggs on foliage close to aphid colonies, or even on plants that are likely to be colonised by aphids.

The larvae resemble the Star Wars character Jabba the Hut, and sort of worm their way around plants, piercing aphids with their mouth hooks, before sucking out the aphids' innards. A single larva can eat up to 200 aphids before it pupates. They're mainly active at night, and are occasionally cannibalistic, eating smaller larvae. The pupal case resembles a pear drop, and may be found stuck to the leaves of plants.

HOW TO ATTRACT THEM: grow a range of flowering plants and ensure there's a plentiful supply of aphids.

6. BLUE BOTTLE, *Calliphora*

Blue bottles have big red eyes and a metallic blue abdomen with black markings. They feed on nectar as well as carrion, and can pollinate strong-scented flowers such as golden rod. The larvae feed on faeces and carcasses of dead animals, before pupating in soil. Adults emerge after two or three weeks and are ready to mate within hours.

Blue bottles might not be the most obvious species you'd want to attract to your garden, but they play an important role, helping clear decaying matter. They're also food for spiders, amphibians, birds and bats. While it's a good idea to prevent blue bottles from landing on your food, there's no reason why they shouldn't be welcomed into your garden.

HOW TO ATTRACT THEM: grow strong-scented flowers and compost waste.

7. COMMON YELLOW DUNG FLY, *Scathophaga stercoraria*

The common yellow dung fly is prettier than you'd think. Adult males are golden yellow and slightly furry, while females are a little duller. They mostly predate smaller flies, but will also visit flowers and may be observed waiting on flowers to hunt prey. Males also prey on blow flies (such as blue bottles) when visiting dung.

Females lay their eggs in dung and are very fussy when it comes to choosing the right spot. To prevent her eggs becoming waterlogged or drying out, she lays on small 'hills' on the dung's surface. The eggs hatch into predatory larvae, which eat other insect larvae within the dung. They feed for up to three weeks before pupating in the soil and eventually emerging as adults.

HOW TO ATTRACT THEM: a good way to lure them in is to make an organic plant food using water and nettle or comfrey leaves. Otherwise, grow a range of nectar-rich flowers.

BUGS

Contrary to the belief that 'bug' is just another name for a creepy crawly, a bug is actually an insect in the order Hemiptera, as a beetle is to the order Coleoptera. Many bugs look a lot like beetles, but they all have a straw-like sucking mouthpart called a beak or rostrum, whereas beetles have mandibles for chewing. Your garden and pond are probably full of bugs without you even noticing (take a look in the Pondlife section, p. 89, for more bugs), but here are just two that are commonly found and easy to recognise.

Ten things to do for bugs
1. Plant a hedge, including hawthorn, which may attract the hawthorn shield bug
2. Grow soft fruit, such as raspberries and blackberries
3. Grow a patch of nettles
4. Grow a variety of herbaceous plants
5. Let a patch of grass grow long or sow a meadow
6. Make a log pile (bury some of the logs in the ground if you can)
7. Sweep fallen leaves under your hedge or gather them in a bespoke wire cage
8. Mulch borders with leafmould
9. Tolerate 'weeds', such as sorrel and dock
10. Grow a range of flowering plants

1. GREEN SHIELD BUG, *Palomena prasina*
The green shield bug is one of a number of bugs named for their shield-like shape (though they are sometimes known as 'stink bugs', owing to the odour they release if handled). Adults are broad, flat and green with a brown 'tail'. In autumn they develop more subdued browny-bronze colourings, possibly to blend in with their surroundings.

Adults feed by sucking sap from a wide range of plants but generally don't cause any damage. They

Left: The nymph of a green shield bug negotiates a rosemary leaf.
Right: A shield bug nymph rests on a kidney vetch flower.
Opposite: Aphids are making a meal of this rose, while a ladybird larva looks on.

appear in spring and spend a month feeding before mating. Females lay hexagonal batches of greenish eggs on the underside of leaves. The nymphs, or baby shield bugs, are pale green with black markings and a more rounded shape than the adults, and they stay on the plant in little groups. They metamorphose into adults in time to feed themselves up prior to hibernation.

HOW TO ATTRACT THEM: pack your garden with foliage.

2. APHIDS

Aphids are the scourge of gardeners, despised for distorting plant growth and excreting a sticky substance that attracts ants and sooty mould. Yet they are some of the most important insects to have in the garden.

They suck sap from plants, piercing the stems and foliage using their beak, or rostrum. Some,

such as the blackfly, *Aphis fabae*, attack a wide range of plants, while others, including the nettle aphid, *Microlophium carnosum*, only eat one plant (in this case, nettles). But look what eats them: ladybirds and their larvae, birds and their babies, parasitic wasps, hoverfly larvae and lacewings. So be nice to aphids. To give aphids a home in your garden is to provide food for countless other species.

HOW TO ATTRACT THEM: grow a wide range of plants, including nettles, beans, roses and clematis.

PONDLIFE

One of the best things about having a pond is the variety of wildlife you'll attract. As well as amphibians and the odd reptile, you'll find countless other creatures inhabiting the watery world beneath the surface.

LOOK OUT FOR:

Dragonflies and damselflies – these magnificent creatures have barely changed in 300 million years, which is a good thing as they have lovely smiling faces. Dragonflies are bigger and more robust-looking than damselflies. They rest with their wings at right angles, like fighter planes. Damselflies are more slender and dainty, are rarely found away from water and rest with their wings shut.

Lifecycle – Both species breed in water, such as ponds, but some prefer canals, rivers and peat bogs. The larvae are predatory, although, again, damselfly larvae are more slender and delicate than their cousins.

Waterboatmen and pondskaters – these bugs are often the first to colonise a new pond – you might spot them flying in on warm summer days. Many are predatory, eating a variety of insects and their larvae. Waterboatmen, *Corixa sp*, which actually spend most of their time at the bottom of the pond, are vegetarian.

Lifecycle – mating takes place between December and May and eggs are laid singly among the stems of water plants. The nymphs take just two months to become adults. Male waterboatmen are said to have the loudest mating calls in the world – which they achieve by rubbing their penis against the abdomen.

Ten things to do for pond life

1. Dig a pond (as large as you have space for) with gentle sloping sides
2. Grow lots of aquatic vegetation
3. Avoid adding fish
4. Add a log or two
5. Ensure there are plenty of flies in the garden, for dragonflies
6. If you need to clear the pond, do so in autumn, to cause the least disturbance
7. Create basking sites, using rocks or large stones
8. Add sticks or grow tall, emergent plants to act as perches for damselflies and dragonflies
9. Remove large amounts of blanketweed by hand, as this can block light
10. Avoid topping up the pond with tap water

1. COMMON DARTER, *Sympetrum striolatum*

If you have dragonflies visiting your garden pond, you'll almost certainly see the common darter. The orange-red males are easiest to spot; whereas females are more of a yellow brown. You'll often see territorial males perched in prominent positions from which they dart after intruders, before returning to exactly the same spot.

Like all dragonflies, the common darter eats a variety of insects, including mosquitoes, midges, small moths and flies. As it moves closer to its prey it uses its front legs to form a 'basket', which scoops up its quarry. But it always returns to its perch to eat.

Mating takes place near water and egg-laying is a double-act, with the male pushing the female downwards so that her abdomen breaks the water's surface.

HOW TO ATTRACT THEM: dig a pond and plant it with a variety of submerged and emergent plants.

2. AZURE DAMSELFLY, *Coenagrion puella*

Blue damselflies are hard to tell apart, but it can be done, with patience. Identifying the azure blue from the common blue depends on observing the markings on the second abdominal segment – male azures have a flat-bottomed U shape, while common damselflies have more of a lollipop shape.

The azure flies from May to September. Males are almost electric blue with a variety of black markings, while females are either blue or green. Mating takes place in summer and eggs are laid on plants just below the water's surface.

HOW TO ATTRACT THEM: dig a pond – the larger the better – in a sunny spot in the garden. Plant it with a variety of submerged and emergent plants to provide the best possible shelter for the larvae.

3. BACKSWIMMER, *Notonecta glauca*

The backswimmer, or greater water boatmen, is a true bug that resembles a boat with a large pair of oars (these are actually its hind legs). Unlike lesser waterboatmen, it swims on its back just under the pond's surface, trapping air under the water using its wings and hairy body.

It might look like a funny little boat, but it's actually a dangerous predator. Adults seek out tadpoles and water beetle larvae using their large eyes, and detect vibrations made by drowning insects with the many hairs on their bodies. Mating takes place between December and May and eggs are laid singly among the stems of water plants. The nymphs take just two months to become adults.

HOW TO ATTRACT THEM: dig a pond with lots of shallow margins and submerged plants.

4. POND SKATER, *Gerris lacustris*

The pond skater has a thin, brownish-grey body and a small head with large eyes. It has three pairs of legs, each with its own function: the first pair is used for grasping prey, the middle pair propels it along the water surface with either a rowing or jumping motion, and the hind pair acts as a set of rudders. Like the backswimmer, the pond skater is also covered in tiny sensitive hairs, which detect vibrations from struggling insects on the pond's surface.

Adults emerge from hibernation in April and May and mating takes place almost immediately. The second generation emerges about a month later. Between November and April, pond skaters leave the pond to hibernate. They sometimes do this in groups, often taking shelter in garden sheds or outhouses.

HOW TO ATTRACT THEM: dig a pond with lots of shallow margins and submerged plants.

This female lies at the centre of her web, waiting for prey to become entangled.

CREEPY CRAWLIES

They're some of the ugliest garden inhabitants, which are often nocturnal and hide away in the darkest corners of our gardens. Some of them are pests, others eat pests and a few are just mistaken for pests. But, they're also some of the most important garden species. Where would we be without earthworms, centipedes and spiders?

Ten things to do for creepy crawlies

1. Dig a pond
2. Compost waste
3. Let an area of grass grow long
4. Create overwintering sites by mulching borders and making piles of leaves
5. Make a log pile
6. Sweep fallen leaves under your hedge or gather them in a bespoke wire cage
7. Create areas of densely planted vegetation
8. Grow as many deciduous trees as you can
9. Plant a hedge
10. Avoid tidying the herbaceous borders in autumn

1. GARDEN SPIDER, *Araneus diadematus*

The garden spider is rarely spotted outside of the months of August and September, when adults suddenly turn up large webs spun across paths and in sizeable shrubs.

It ranges in colour from light yellow to dark grey, but always has mottled markings across the back with five or more large, white dots forming a cross. Females are larger than males. The web is spun by the female, which usually lies on it head down, waiting for prey to become entangled.

The web also provides a platform on which to mate, although the male approaches cautiously. After mating, the female builds a silken sac in which to lay her eggs and then spends the rest of her life looking after them. She dies in late autumn, and her spiderlings hatch out the following May.

2. HARVESTMEN

Harvestmen are related to spiders and look superficially like them, but they don't have a clearly defined waist, so they can be told apart from spiders by the appearance of having just one, small body. They typically have much longer legs than spiders, too.

Harvestmen don't build webs, have fangs or the ability to produce venom, but prey on a variety of invertebrates using the hooks on their legs. Unlike spiders, they can chew food, and can defend themselves against predators by releasing a foul smell. They can even shed a leg or two to escape.

3. COMMON EARWIG, *Forficula auricularia* The name 'earwig' comes from the old English word 'earwicga' which means 'ear beetle', as it was once thought that they burrowed into people's ears at night to lay eggs in their brains. They're very unlikely to do such a thing.

The common earwig is small, shiny and brown with distinctive tail pincers. It's often regarded as a pest, as it nibbles dahlia and chrysanthemum flowers, but it also eats decaying plant material, carrion and other insects, including aphids. Adults hunt at night and hide by day, where they can be found under logs and stones and in damp crevices.

The loveliest thing about earwigs is that the females are good mothers. They lay twenty to thirty eggs under stones and in crevices, which they protect from predators and gently clean. After the nymphs have hatched, their mother stays with them until they're big enough to fend for themselves.

4. EARTHWORM

There are lots of different types of earthworm, all of which recycle decaying matter into valuable humus. In doing so they aerate the soil, aid drainage and make nutrients more available to plants. They're also food for hedgehogs, badgers, birds and amphibians.

They live in a variety of habitats, depending on the species. The thin, reddish brandling worm,

Opposite: A garden spider rests on a web suspended between thistles. **Above:** This worm is putting itself in danger of being eaten, by travelling across grass.

Eisenia fetida, is found in large numbers in compost heaps and leaf piles, while larger, pinker worms such as the garden earthworm, *Lumbricus terrestris*, live beneath lawns and borders. If you go out at night with a torch you may see leaves being pulled beneath the soil surface by worms.

Worms are hermaphrodite. Breeding takes place in summer with an exchange of sperm, then each worm lays a cocoon of eggs in the soil.

5. BLACK ANT, *Lasius niger*

The black ant is one of a number of ant species we might find in our gardens, and lives in large colonies like social bees and wasps. Colonies can last for up to several years, with workers bringing food back to the nest for the grubs.

Ants don't tend to be loved by gardeners. They sometimes make nests in inconvenient spots like compost bins and plant pots, and they have an annoying habit of farming aphids for their honeydew and protecting them from predators. Sometimes they turn up in kitchen cupboards.

But they also eat caterpillars and other insects and are themselves food for common toads, lizards and birds, including the green woodpecker which pretty much only eats ants. On Flying Ants Day, when thousands take to the sky to mate and establish new colonies, gulls, swallows and starlings have a feast.

Ants patrol an aphid colony, milking the blackfly for honeydew, and warding off predators.

Millipede.

6. WOODLICE, CENTIPEDES AND MILLIPEDES

Woodlice are found in compost heaps and rotting wood, and are sometimes blamed for damage to strawberry crops (which is more likely to have been done by slugs). They're crustaceans and there are lots of different types, some of which can roll into a ball when threatened.

They eat decaying organic matter, including dead leaves, and they're predated by spiders, shrews, toads and some birds.

Centipedes are voracious carnivores, which predate on spiders, worms, caterpillars and snails. Millipedes, which sometimes look like woodlice, eat decaying plant matter.

3

Plants

To you and me, a garden packed with plants is a garden packed with beauty. Plants provide structure, colour, texture, scent and sound. A tree provides something to sit under or even climb. But to wildlife, plants represent food and shelter every day of the year. What we grow and how we grow it determines how much food and shelter is available.

A YEAR IN THE LIFE OF GARDEN PLANTS

Spring

In early spring, bumblebee queens cling to unopened crocuses, waiting for a sunny day to open the flowers and release their life-giving nectar. As temperatures increase, butterflies, caterpillars and other insects stir from the shelter of a piece of bark, leaf pile or thicket of ivy, and hedgehogs make their first foray of the year looking for the insects that rely on all of these plants. As spring draws to a close, birds scour gardens for moss, lichens, bits of twig and fallen leaves to build their nests, and the first babies of the year are born.

Summer

The number of insects increases: bumblebee nests grow as workers collect pollen and nectar for their siblings. Soldier beetles stake out flowers for a mate and the caterpillars of butterflies and moths nibble leaves before pupating. Tiny eggs are laid on foliage, in hollow plant stems and dead wood, while the folded leaves of pond plants protect newt eggs. Birds and wasps prey on aphids and caterpillars; ants fight ladybirds to farm aphids for their honeydew. Towards the end of summer, male bumblebees rub their scent on leaves to attract daughter queens, and the second generation of butterflies emerges.

Autumn

Insect activity changes: small tortoiseshell and red admiral butterflies crowd together on buddleia flowers and drink nectar to fatten themselves up for hibernation or the long flight back to warmer climes. Bumblebee and wasp nests break down, as mated daughter queens find a piece of bark or thicket of ivy to protect them while they hibernate. Recently fledged birds pick the last of the insects off trees, and amphibians take shelter in log piles and compost heaps. Hedgehogs bury themselves under a thick duvet of fallen leaves.

Winter

Spent foliage in our borders protects insects, amphibians and mammals from frost and damp conditions. Blackbirds pick over fallen leaves for hibernating insects while migrant redwings and fieldfares join hundreds of other birds in the hunt for winter berries. A thick hedge provides a frost-free roost and protects birds and small mammals

Opposite: Bird's-foot trefoil adds a splash of colour.

from predators. After the shortest day, bird activity gradually takes on a renewed vigour and by late winter the first of the spring bulbs are beginning to push through the soil.

WHAT TO GROW

We've already looked at pond plants, plants for pollinators, caterpillar foodplants and fruiting plants and trees for birds (see pp. 29). Grow the widest selection possible and you'll be well on your way to having a noisy, bustling garden, a circus of leaf munchers, wood borers, nectar drinkers and everything else that makes up the exciting web of life that's possible outside the back door.

We've also looked at dead plants: making compost heaps and log and leaf piles for detrivores, reptiles, amphibians and hedgehogs. So what's missing?

WEEDS

Unfortunately, not all wildlife-friendly plants are beautiful cultivars, resplendent with ornate flowers and jewel-like berries or seeds. Some are a bit ugly. Others are extremely pernicious, spreading like wildfire the minute your back is turned. Yet these plants, or weeds, are often fantastic for wildlife. Not only are some of them so successful that you'll find them growing almost anywhere, but most have been here for millennia, evolving with the wildlife.

That said, weeds aren't necessary in the wildlife garden, but some can enhance it. Perhaps you have an area out of sight where you can tolerate a few, or you can appreciate the beauty of some, such as self-heal and bird's foot trefoil, in your lawn. After all, a weed is just a plant growing in the wrong place. Find the right place, and the wildlife will love you.

The following list comprises ten plants which are commonly regarded as weeds. All of them are fantastic for wildlife and, with the exception of bramble, are fairly easy to remove should you need to. Many weeds thrive in lawns. You can enable these plants to flower by simply mowing less often or raising the height of your mower blade. Prevent them from spreading to ornamental borders by cutting them down as soon as they've flowered.

Top Ten Weeds

1. BIRD'S FOOT TREFOIL, *Lotus corniculatus*
Bird's foot trefoil is an excellent source of pollen and nectar for bees, and the foliage for caterpillars of the common blue butterfly and six-spotted burnet moth. It's a common lawn weed, so probably already grows in your lawn.

2. BRAMBLE, *Rubus fruiticosus*
A patch of brambles is well worth growing if you can afford the space. Moth caterpillars eat the leaves, bees and butterflies visit the flowers and birds, dormice and butterflies feast on the berries. A dense thicket also provides shelter for hedgehogs and nesting birds.

3. CHICKWEED, *Stellaria media*
Nearly every garden is home to chickweed, which is fast growing and self seeds easily. The foliage is popular with moth caterpillars and finches eat its seeds. It's also edible, and is delicious in salads. Simply remove any plants growing in the wrong place.

4. SPEAR THISTLE, *Cirsium vulgare*
The wildlife value of the spear thistle is exceptional. Caterpillars of many species of butterfly and moth, including the painted lady, feed on its foliage, and the flowers are a fantastic source of pollen and nectar. Goldfinches eat the seeds.

Kidney vetch and self-heal.

White clover flowers in a lawn.

A small copper takes nectar from a bramble flower.

5. DANDELION, *Taraxacum officinale*

The dandelion is the larval foodplant for a number of moths, including the white ermine and large yellow underwing. Its flowers are a rich source of nectar and pollen for pollinators, and goldfinches eat the seeds.

6. RAGWORT, *Senecio jacobaea*

As well as providing a fantastic source of nectar and pollen, ragwort is food for nearly eighty insect species, of which more than thirty depend on it, including the beautiful cinnabar moth. It can be poisonous if eaten by animals, especially horses, so avoid growing it if you live near grazing land.

7. ROSEBAY WILLOWHERB, *Epilobium angustifolium*

It's well worth tolerating a small patch of rosebay willowherb, if only for the chance of encouraging the amazing elephant hawk-moth to lay her eggs. Bees and butterflies also visit the flowers. It's fairly easy to control, simply remove seedheads before they disperse.

8. SELF-HEAL, *Prunella vulgaris*

This low-growing, spreading weed is common in sunny lawns. Bees and butterflies love its beautiful, rich purple flowers. It may well already be growing in your lawn.

9. STINGING NETTLE, *Urtica diocia*

The leaves are eaten by the nettle aphid, the nettle weevil, numerous moth larvae and of course the caterpillars of many garden butterflies. Birds, including bullfinches, eat the seeds. If you have the space and inclination, grow them in the sunniest spot possible.

10. WHITE CLOVER, *Trifolium repens*

Clover is an excellent source of pollen and nectar for pollinators, particularly bees. Like self-heal and bird's foot trefoil, it's probably already growing in your lawn.

STINGING NETTLES

Because they have stinging hairs, and are therefore avoided by most grazing animals, nettles are home to more than forty species of insect – many of which are beautiful garden butterflies and moths. They're also host to the nettle aphid, which emerges earlier in spring than other species of aphid, providing an important source of food for ladybirds. In late summer, birds eat the seeds.

Not every garden is suitable for a nettle patch but, if you do decide to grown them, don't do things by halves. Grow as big a patch as you can afford, in full sun. It's thought that some butterflies won't breed on small, shady clumps (though some species of moth, and of course ladybirds, will). If you can, take seeds or dig up a clump from a patch growing nearby, so you have local nettles, for local insects. The wildlife will love you.

Mosses and Liverworts

These are primitive plants, or bryophytes, and grow in places other plants don't. They're often the first to colonise new spaces, greening roofs and walls that would otherwise remain bare. Along with other 'pioneer species' such as algae, lichens and some weeds, mosses and liverworts take advantage of the lack of competition from taller plants, creating new habitats for invertebrates and ultimately a growing medium for tree seedlings.

There are hundreds of different species, some of which are suited to growing in lawns, while others form on hard surfaces, like paths, greenhouse glazing, walls and garden ornaments. They take different forms, with mosses often appearing as large tufts or compact cushions, and liverworts tending to grow in flatter, fleshier clumps.

They thrive in shady, damp conditions, and can compete with grass in poorly drained lawns. Moss is particularly useful to birds, which will scour your garden in spring, taking lumps back to line their nests.

TIP: To remove moss from your lawn, you need to improve the growing conisations. Use a spring-tined rake to remove thatch, aerate the lawn by spiking it with a garden fork and top dress with a (preferably organic) lawn feed every autumn. This should create the conditions suited for growing grass, rather than moss.

Lichen

Lichens are part algae, part fungi. There are thousands of different types, most of which need clean, unpolluted air to grow. They grow anywhere, colonising bare stone, bird tables, paths, twigs and roof slates. They come in a variety of different colours, from the glorious yellow *Xanthoria parietina* to the sea-green *Flavoparmelia caperata*. Caterpillars of some moths, including the marble beauty, *Cryphia domestica*, and scarce footman, *Eilema complana*, eat lichens, and some birds decorate their nests with them.

Fungi

Fungi is neither a plant nor animal. There are lots of different types, most of which are beneficial in gardens. Fungi can't photosynthesise as plants do, so they derive their nutrients by breaking down plant and animal material, in turn helping to turn organic matter into humus, aiding soil structure. Some fungi are parasites, specialising in live plant material. Ohers are saprophytes, living off dead matter.

Many plants have a mutually beneficial relationship with fungi, which attach to the plants' roots, helping them absorb nutrients. Wood mice are partial to eating some species.

Trees

Trees also deserve a special mention, providing food and shelter for hundreds and hundreds of species. Not every garden has room for a large tree, such as an oak, but most plots have space for an apple or goat willow, which are extremely valuable to wildlife.

Ten trees for wildlife

It's hard to pull out just ten trees from the hundreds we could grow in our gardens, as plants that cater for one species might not be so good for another. Here, I've listed those that provide food and shelter for a wide variety of species.

Virtually all of the following trees are good for moths. This is because there are thousands of

Opposite: Mosses have colonised this slate roof, growing in large green cushions. **Above:** Lichen and navelwort grow on a stone wall. **Right:** Pleated inkcap mushrooms poke through the grass in a lawn.

species, some of which favour specific trees and others that eat virtually anything. But the more moths you can bring to your garden, the more birds and bats you'll feed, too.

1. APPLE, *Malus*
Ideal for smaller gardens, apple trees provides leaves for moths, flowers for bees and fruit for birds. The bark is colonised by lichens and is a fantastic host to mistletoe, providing further berries for birds. Cultivated apples seem to be just as good. Height 3–6m.

2. BEECH, *Fagus sylvatica*
Can be grown as a tree in large gardens, or a hedge in smaller plots. Hedge-grown plants retain their autumn leaves, providing shelter for birds. Many moths eat the leaves and birds and small mammals eat the seed (beechmast) in autumn. Height 10–35m.

3. COMMON HAWTHORN, *Crataegus monogyna*
Grown as part of a hedge, the common hawthorn provides the perfect nesting and roosting opportunities for birds. Bees love the flowers, while moths and the hawthorn shield bug love the foliage. The berries are an important source of winter food. Height 12–15m.

4. FIELD MAPLE, *Acer campestre*
This is perfect for small gardens, as it can be trimmed into a hedge. Lichens and mosses grow on the bark; moths eat the foliage and bees and wasps visit the spring flowers. In autumn the leaves turn a lovely golden colour. Height 8–14m.

5. GOAT WILLOW, *Salix caprea*
Of all willow species, this is probably the best for wildlife. The catkins provide an early source of food for bees, and moths, aphids and other insects eat the foliage. Choose the popular cultivar 'Kilmarnock' for tiny gardens, as it grows to just 2m. Height 6–10m.

6. HAZEL, *Corylus avellana*
Hazel is a fantastic, dense hedging plant that's ideal for small gardens. The foliage is popular with moths, and the catkins provide an early source of food for bees. Squirrels, dormice, great-spotted woodpeckers and nuthatches eat the nuts. Height 12–15m.

7. LIME, *Tilia cordata* or *T. playphyllos*
Only really suitable for large garden. Leaves are eaten by aphids and moth caterpillars including the spectacular lime hawk-moth, flowers are pollinated by bees and the seeds are occasionally eaten by birds. The grooved bark provides hibernation opportunities for insects. Height 20–40m.

8. OAK, *Quercus robur*
Probably the best tree for wildlife, but only if you have a large garden. A mature tree provides shelter and nesting opportunities for birds, acorns for birds and small mammals, leaves for moths and aphids and crevices for spiders. Height 15–25m.

9. SILVER BIRCH, *Betula pendula*
A beautiful and busy tree to grow in the garden, the silver birch is popular with moths, beetles, bugs and sawflies, and therefore blue tits and other insect eaters. Finches eat the seeds, too. It's slow growing and can be controlled with regular pruning. Height 18–25m.

10. YEW, *Taxus baccata*
Several yews can be grown into a beautiful dense hedge, making the perfect nesting and roosting site for birds. The leaves and seeds are toxic, but the flesh of the berries is not, enabling thrushes to disperse the seed without being harmed. Height 4—20m.

Climbing Plants

The more climbing plants you can grow up your walls and fences, the more shelter you provide. But on top of shelter, some climbers provide nectar and pollen, foliage for caterpillars and berries for birds. Here are five no garden should be without:

Top five climbing plants

1. CLEMATIS, *Clematis*

Many varieties are unsuitable for wildlife, although their foliage provides shelter. Better cultivars include *Clematis cirrhosa*, 'Freckles', which produces nectar-rich flowers in late winter. The most wildlife-friendly is old man's beard, *Clematis vitalba*, which offers scrubby shelter, moth food and lovely fluffy seedheads. Height 30m.

2. HONEYSUCKLE, *Lonicera periclymenum*

This beautiful, scented climber provides food for long-tongued bumblebees and large moths. Some moths also eat the foliage, while birds eat the sticky red berries. It can be prone to mildew, but grows best given a deep root run in partial shade. Height up to 7m.

3. IVY, *Hedera helix*

Mature (arboreal) ivy flowers when most other plants have stopped blooming, and has plenty of nooks and crannies to shelter nesting birds and insects. Birds eat the calorie-rich berries. The foliage provides food for caterpillars of the holly blue butterfly as well as moths. Height 10m.

4. ROSE, *Rosa*

Lots of roses are fantastic for wildlife, but others are not so good. As well as field rose, *Rosa arvensis*, and dog rose, *Rosa canina*, aim for open, single-flowered cultivars such as 'Kew Gardens' and 'Rambling Rector'. Double-flowered 'Madame Alfred Carrière' and 'Golden Showers' are apparently popular with leafcutter bees. Height up to 6m.

5. WISTERIA, *Wisteria floribunda, W. sinensis*

Wisteria is a great choice for covering east-facing walls, producing beautiful nectar-rich flowers. Most cultivars have purple flowers, but white-flowered varieties are available. Birds such as blackbirds and robins nest among the branches. Height 9m.

4

Trouble Shooter

Wild creatures don't always read the books, or follow the rules. Some come in to our gardens when we'd really rather they didn't; others indulge in strange behaviour we don't recognise or understand; and then there are those which are in trouble and simply need our help. This troubleshooting guide is aimed at helping you understand the weird ways, deal with unwelcome guests and recognise cries for help, so you can act quickly.

SPRING

Help! I've seen a rat

Most gardens will have a rat passing through from time to time, but problems can arise when they decide to set up home. They tend to gather in groups and can breed at a phenomenal rate. Many carry Weil's disease in their urine, which can cause jaundice and occasionally even be fatal to humans, and they're also expert tunnellers, so may easily gain access to your house.

What can I do? Deter them by fixing trays to your hanging bird feeders to prevent spilled food from falling on the ground, and only leave small quantities at a time on ground feeders. Storing bird food in metal, airtight containers will also help. You can prevent access to your compost bin by fixing sturdy chicken wire to the bottom. If the problem gets worse or doesn't improve, call in the experts.

There's a large bumblebee on my windowsill. It's barely moving

This is likely to be a bumblebee queen, which can be drowsy when they emerge from hibernation and need energy to help them fly to find and establish a new nest. She's extremely unlikely to sting you, so gently pick her up on the end of your finger or a piece of card and pop her on a flower such as a crocus or hellebore. If there are no flowers available, half fill a shallow bottle top with a mixture made from 1tsp sugar with 2tsp water and place next to the bee. She should start drinking from it immediately, and will be ready to fly within a few minutes.

SUMMER

I've found a grounded swift. It can't fly

Due to their long wings and short legs, all but the strongest swifts are unable to launch themselves into flight from the ground. So if a baby falls out of the nest it will perish unless found by a helpful gardener.

What can I do? If it's an adult and you think it can fly, simply hold it in the palms of your hands and raise your hands high in the air. Make sure you're releasing the bird into the wind and choose a place where, if it comes straight back down, you can find it. If it's really thin or a baby that's fallen before it's able to fly, it will need caring for before it can be released. Swifts are very hard to care for so need to be looked after by experts. Pick it up and pop it in a box with a lid on it, so it can settle down, and contact your local bird group or society for help (see p. 108 for details).

There's a baby bird on my lawn. Should I take it in and care for it?

No. The parents are usually very close by and it's very unlikely that they've abandoned their baby. The young of many species fledge after they've grown feathers but before they can fly, so the baby could just be spending a couple of days on the ground before it's ready to take to the sky.

What can I do? If you have a cat, keep it indoors until the bird has flown. If you think the bird is in a particularly vulnerable position then you can move it to a more appropriate place, but don't move it too far away or the parents won't be able to find it (touching a bird won't make its parents abandon it). Otherwise, just keep an eye on it. If the parents don't return, call your local wildlife rescue centre (for details see p. 108).

Where have all the birds gone?

After breeding, many garden birds moult. During this period they're less able to escape from predators, so they lie low until they've grown their winter plumage. There's also an abundance of natural food in the trees, fields and hedgerows in late summer, as grain, berries and fruit ripen. So the birds are less dependent on your garden.

What can I do? Nothing, they will soon be back, although this might be the perfect opportunity to give feeders a good clean.

I've found a dead greenfinch in the garden

This could be the result of trichomoniasis, which affects the upper digestive tract of greenfinches and collard doves, making it hard for the birds to eat. Eventually they die of starvation.

What can I do? Sweep up and dispose of any spilled food and empty, clean and disinfect your feeders. It's also a good idea to stop feeding for at least a month.

How can I stop my cat from killing local wildlife?

Cats kill millions of small mammals and birds every year, and they also like to catch, play with and sometimes kill bats and frogs.

What can I do? Fix a collar and bell to your cat so birds and small mammals can hear it coming. Bring your cat indoors before sunset and keep it in until an hour after sunset (all night if possible), between April and October, especially between mid-June and the end of August when bats are caring for their babies.

I've found a bat on the ground, does it need help?

Probably, yes. Bats come to ground when they are exhausted and starving – often during cold, wet summers when insects are in short supply.

What can I do? Use a glove or cloth to put the bat in a box with kitchen paper in the bottom, a small soft cloth and a tin lid of water. Phone the Bat Conservation Trust Helpline for details of your nearest bat carer (see p. 108).

Help! I've disturbed a hedgehog's nest

Some hedgehog mothers will abandon or kill their young, while others may just move them to a new location, or even settle back down if the nest hasn't been disturbed too much. It's hard to say.

What can I do? Try to replace as much nesting material as you can and don't disturb the nest again. Place a twig or leaf over the entrance, which the mother will have to brush aside, so you can tell if she is still making regular trips to and from the nest.

It's also a good idea to pop a dish each of water and meat-based dog or cat food outside, so she doesn't have to travel far in order to replace energy to suckle her young. If the mum doesn't appear to be returning to the nest, or if you hear squeaking from within, then the hoglets need to be rescued. Call you local hedgehog carer for advice (see p. 108 for details).

What's wrong with my frogs?

Since the 1980s, a devastating virus has swept through the UK, killing frogs and other amphibians, as well as reptiles. The virus is thought to have come from America and is most noticeable in mid-summer. Frogs display a range of symptoms, ranging from a reddening of the skin (the virus is sometimes called 'red leg'), ulcers, haemorrhaging, drowsiness, emaciation and eye problems. Most people simply just find a large number of dead frogs in their garden.

What can I do? There's no cure at the moment, but the virus does pass through frog populations and they do recover after an outbreak. Some research has suggested that some frogs are resistant to the disease. The best thing to do is contact the Frog Mortality Project (details on p. 108), which is conducting research into the disease. Avoid spreading the disease by digging a deep hole to bury the bodies.

AUTUMN

I've just seen a hedgehog out during the day. I thought they were nocturnal?

Hedgehogs are primarily nocturnal, but nesting mothers may be seen out during the day in spring, gathering materials or even moving their babies to a more suitable nest site. However, if you see a hedgehog lying down during the day, it could be an orphaned baby or injured, poisoned or just cold.

A hedgehog foraging during the day in autumn is likely to be a late-born baby which hasn't gained enough weight in order to survive hibernation. As each autumn day passes, natural food sources such as caterpillars and slugs are in ever decreasing supply, so the hedgehog's chances of survival are slim.

Unless it's a mother hedgehog taking a short break from her nest during the day, it's likely to be in trouble. If it's particularly small, or you find a hedgehog lying down or staggering about, it needs immediate help.

What can I do? Take it in and keep it warm. Pop it on a hot water bottle wrapped in a towel, in a high-sided box lined with newspaper, and then place another towel over the hedgehog to make it feel secure. Ensure the bottle is kept warm. Offer it some water and meat-based dog or cat food. If the hedgehog doesn't take the food or it's injured, call your local hedgehog carer or Hedgehog Society for advice (see p. 108 for details).

Help! Badgers keep digging up my lawn!

Badgers mainly eat worms and insect larvae, and can dig up lawns looking for leatherjackets and chafer grubs. It's not a problem if they're just eating worms, which they merely suck out of the ground, but they use their paws to dig out grubs, leaving big muddy patches in the sward. Digging activity and damage tend to peak in autumn. Some gardeners tolerate this as an aesthetic compromise for having badgers in the garden. Others would rather have a nice lawn.

What can I do? The easiest way to solve the problem is to scatter peanuts over the area, which the badgers will eat instead of digging for grubs (it's also lovely to watch). But, if this is a huge problem and you really want a long-term solution, you need to remove the larvae that attract the badgers. You can deter craneflies and chafers from laying eggs by regularly mowing, removing moss and aerating the lawn. You can also apply nematodes, which safely kill the grubs without harming other wildlife.

Why are ladybirds coming into my house?

Two-spots and harlequins are the most likely species to come into houses. They turn up in autumn looking to hibernate, and release a hormone to attract others to join them. Sometimes hundreds of ladybirds can gather in the same spot. In cool rooms they just settle down for winter and disappear again in April, but in heated rooms they don't settle and can fly around the room, stain furniture and even bite people. Due to being active but unable to eat, many die.

What can I do? If you're happy to share your home with them, then let them get on with it but do try to turn the heating off in the room they're sheltering in. If you'd rather they spent winter elsewhere, gather them up in a shoe box or similar, and pop them somewhere cool and dry such as your shed or garage. Make sure they can escape in spring.

My pond is full of leaves. Will it harm wildlife?

Yes and no. The best ponds have a bit of natural sediment at the bottom, including fallen leaves, twigs and branches. Indeed, fallen leaves make a good habitat for hibernating frogs and even a nice coat for caddisfly larvae. However, a large amount of leaf fall in ponds isn't ideal, as it can upset the pH balance of the water and contribute to the build up of noxious gasses under ice (which can kill any frogs at the bottom).

What can I do? Try to achieve a balance. If you do decide to clear out your pond, do so in autumn, as this causes the least disturbance to wildlife. There's no need to change the water, simply use a net to retrieve leaves from the surface (or the bottom, if you think there are too many), and let the water settle back down. If you need to make repairs to your pond, try to collect as much water as you can and return it to the pond when you've finished. Any aquatic larvae can also be rescued and returned. Do make piles of collected leaves around the pond for any creatures to crawl back into the pond, and do double-check for stragglers before popping the leaves on the compost.

Why are there still tadpoles in my pond?

Tadpoles have usually developed into young adults by mid-summer, but it's not uncommon to find tadpoles in the pond in autumn. Reasons could include a lack of food due to a particularly large amount of spawn laid, or cold water due to a lack of light reaching the pond. If the tadpoles survive winter they will complete their development and leave the pond in spring.

What can I do? If the pond is in the shade, consider cutting back any trees or shrubs that block the light, as this will help the water maintain a warmer temperature next year. Avoid providing tadpoles with extra food now, as this could mean they complete their development in mid-winter, when natural sources of food in the garden are in short supply.

WINTER

There are two foxes stuck together in my garden – they've been there for hours

Don't worry, this is perfectly normal, if perhaps a little frustrating for the foxes. There can be a bit of swelling after mating, causing the dog fox and vixen to lock together, known as a 'tie'. Unable to dismount, the male swings his back leg over the vixen and they wait, back to back for the swelling to go down.

What can I do? Just leave them to it, and try to stay out of the garden until they've vacated.

The ice on my pond has thawed and the water is full of dead frogs

This is extremely distressing, but it's perfectly normal. Frogs (particularly males) spend winter at the bottom of ponds, breathing through their skin. A thick layer of ice can form over the pond during prolonged cold periods, which prevents noxious gases formed as plant debris breaks down from leaving the water. These gases can then poison the frogs, known as 'winterkill'.

What can I do? You can prevent it from happening again by removing some leaf litter and other debris from the pond in autumn. Boil a saucepan of water and rest the pan on the surface of the pond to melt a hole in the ice. (It's easier to do this before a thick layer builds up and you'll need to do this regularly to stop the hole freezing over again.) Never smash the ice, as this can shock and kill any frogs or other creatures in the pond.

Help! I've disturbed a hibernating toad

Don't worry, it will probably be fine. Frogs and toads hibernate in compost bins, logs piles, ditches and the muddy depths of ponds. Disturbing them can expose them to predators, but they should be fine if they're quickly moved.

What can I do? Move the frog or toad to a similar spot, such as a compost heap or log pile, where it can settle down again, and avoid disturbing that area again until spring.

Help! There's a wasp/hornet nest in my garden

Wasps nest in a variety of situations, including bird boxes, lofts and holes in the ground. Hornets (which are incredibly docile, despite their aggressive appearance) tend to inhabit wooded areas, so you may find them nesting in holes in trees or logs. Nests are annual, so the occupants have usually gone by October.

What can I do? The nest needn't be a problem, but it's a good idea to stay out of the flight path of workers leaving the nest, as they may perceive you as a threat and sting you (especially wasps – hornets rarely sting). Otherwise they're unlikely to bother you at all. For more on wasps see p. 70.

There's a butterfly in my house. Will it survive?

Most butterflies and moths overwinter as eggs, larvae or pupae, but some, including the brimstone, comma, peacock and small tortoiseshell, hibernate as adults. They need cool, dry conditions, and the small tortoiseshell and peacock will occasionally come into houses. Unfortunately, when central heating comes on in winter, the butterflies can wake up and waste energy fluttering about.

What can I do? Gently scoop it into a box and pop it in a cool, dry spot such as a shed or garage. Close the box to help the butterfly settle down if it is awake, but do remember to open it again in spring, so it can find its way outside.

List of Wildlife Organisations

Amphibian and Reptile Groups of the UK
arguk.org

Bat Conservation Trust
bats.org.uk

British Dragonfly Society
british-dragonflies.org.uk

British Hedgehog Preservation Society BHPS
britishhedgehogs.org.uk

British Trust for Ornithology
bto.org

Buglife
buglife.org.uk

Bumblebee Conservation Trust
bumblebeeconservation.org

Flora locale
floralocale.org

Froglife
froglife.org

Hawk and owl Trust
hawkandowl.org

Moths Count
mothscount.org

Natural England
naturalengland.org.uk

Red Squirrel Survival Trust
rsst.org.uk

RSPB
rspb.org.uk

Swift Conservation
swift-conservation.org

The Mammal Society
mammal.org.uk

The RHS
rhs.org.uk

The Wildlife Trusts
wildlifetrusts.org

UK Ladybird Survey
ladybird-survey.org

Wild About Gardens
wildaboutgardens.org.uk

WWF UK
wwf.org.uk

Wildlife Gardening Suppliers

Habitat Aid
habitataid.co.uk

Emorsgate seeds
wildseed.co.uk

RSPB shop
shopping.rspb.org.uk

Chiltern Seeds
chilternseeds.co.uk

Chapelwood
chapelwoodwildlife.co.uk

Puddle Plants
puddleplants.co.uk

Really Wild Flowers
reallywildflowers.co.uk

Wiggly Wigglers
wigglywigglers.co.uk

Acknowledgements

I couldn't have written this book without the enormous support of my family, not least mum for letting me dig her a second pond and dad for reading and commenting on vast chunks of copy. Special thanks also to Chris for letting me use her garden as a prop and doing the very important job of being lighting director, Ceals for cooking nourishing dinners and Ellie and Anna for providing alternative conversation ("I don't even know what a newt looks like").

Thank you to my wonderful new agent Jane and everyone at Pen and Sword Books.

Many thanks to Lawrence Arnold for one of the best days of the year at the London Wetland Centre – the smell of grass snake musk will always remind me of your kindness and generosity. We also had a fabulous morning photographing Toady in the garden of Ray and Barbara Cranfield. Thank you to Miles King for reassuring me that ragwort should be included in my list of top 10 weeds and Abigail, Frances and Eden for letting me pimp their shed.

Thank you to the RSPB shop and Chaplewood for generously providing bird food and feeders for shoots, Puddle Plants for supplying pond plants and baskets, and Juliet Blundell of Sedum Green Roof for donating sedum plug plants. Thank you to Lorraine and Nigel from number 33 for giving me a few logs for my log pile project and @DayMoonRoseDawn for the clever idea of using oasis flower foam to make solitary bee habitats.

I would also like to thank the experts who read through my content, in no particular order: Richard Comont, Jules Howard, Mike Toms, Fay Vass, Shirley Thompson, Richard Fox, Les Hill, Ben Darvill, Dave Goulson and Marina Pacheco. You are so talented and knowledgeable and my book would be poorer without you.